MW01713388

The Healthy MILLIONAIRE™

The Secret to Manifesting Health and Wealth

Dr. Janine Bowring, ND

The Healthy Millionaire™

Published in 2008 by Dolce Book Publishing Inc.

Cover Photography: Lisa Mininni
Makeup: Rita Stirpe
Design: Dolce Book Publishing Inc.

For privacy, all patient names have been changed in this publication.

Medical Disclaimer
Content in this publication is provided for informational purposes only, and is not intended as a substitute for the advice provided by your physician or other health-care professional. You should not use the information in this book for diagnosing or treating a health problem or disease, or prescribing any medication or other treatment. You should always speak with your physician or other health-care professional before taking any medication, or nutritional, herbal or homeopathic supplement, or adopting any treatment for a health problem. The author does not assume any liability from the use of information in this publication by any reader.

Publisher's Note
The opinions expressed in this book are those of the author, and do not necessarily reflect the views of the publisher. Although all efforts have been made to ensure accuracy of this work, Dolce Book Publishing Inc. does not assume liability for content, or accuracy of dates, places, names, and citations. The material in this book is intended for information purposes only, and is in no way intended to supersede professional advice.

First edition
National Library of Canada Cataloguing in Publication
The Healthy Millionaire™
Dr. Janine Bowring, ND

ISBN: 978-0-9734656-7-9
Printed in Canada

Dolce Book Publishing Inc.
111 Zenway Blvd., Suite 30, Vaughan, ON L4H 3H9
T: 905.264.6789

In memory of my mother

Success is not the key to happiness. Happiness is the key to success.
If you love what you are doing, you will be successful.

—Albert Schweitzer, humanitarian and medical doctor

TABLE OF CONTENTS

CHAPTER 2: DIET

CHAPTER 3: EXERCISE

CHAPTER 4: ENVIRONMENTAL TOXICITY

CHAPTER 5: HEAVY METAL TOXICITY

CHAPTER 6: CANDIDIASIS AND FUNGAL INFECTIONS

CHAPTER 7: NATUROPATHIC REMEDIES FOR DETOXIFYING THE BODY

CHAPTER 8: DETOXIFICATION OF THE MIND

CHAPTER 9: RELATIONSHIPS

CHAPTER 10: NATUROPATHIC REMEDIES FOR DETOXIFYING THE MIND

CHAPTER 11: THE DETOXIFICATION OF SPIRIT

CHAPTER 12: A SOUL-FULL LIFE

CHAPTER 13: CHAKRAS

CHAPTER 14: NATUROPATHIC REMEDIES FOR DETOXIFYING THE SPIRIT

This powerful guidebook for health and prosperity shows that the relationship between body and mind cannot be separated. In *The Healthy Millionaire*™, Dr. Bowring, ND shows how the detoxification process opens up doors of potential on every level, so that we can prosper in all departments of our life.

Darlene Montgomery
Author/ Creator of *Conscious Women Conscious Lives* book series, and *Dream Yourself Awake: One Woman's Journey to Discover her Divine Mission Using Dreams and Intuition*

PREFACE

Over the years, my practice as a naturopathic doctor has allowed me to get a glimpse into the lives of many successful millionaires, and those aspiring to become millionaires. My perception at one time was that all millionaires knew how to take care of themselves and prevent disease, merely because they were rich. The more I interviewed this group of patients, the more I realized that their health suffered more than most, because they lacked a deeper understanding of the word "health." I also found that toxicity, whether in the physical, emotional or spiritual sphere, was a common cause of disease.

Health, to me, means being happy, physically free from illness and disease, and having a sense of purpose and belonging on this planet. Health is comprised of three dimensions: physical, emotional and spiritual. To be truly healthy, balance and synergy need to exist on all three levels.

Millionaires have a common thread of struggle with acquiring and maintaining this balance of physical, emotional and spiritual health. For this reason, *The Healthy Millionaire™* was created. My belief is that:

Wealth + Health = AFFLUENCE
Wealth + Disease = POVERTY

It is absolutely imperative to be healthy in order to attain and maintain wealth. Ask anyone who is sick if their money matters all that much. Yes, the money may help to pay the medical bills, but most would prefer to have less money in exchange for good health.

This book is for those aspiring to be millionaires, as well as the already successful millionaire. It is a comprehensive guide for those who intend to create and keep their millions, and maintain their health in doing so. It is one thing to create wealth, another to keep it. Sometimes the stress of keeping the wealth can outweigh the difficulty of creating it in the first place. Stress kills. The good news is that, using the tools in this book, disease can be prevented and good health is attainable through detoxification, so that millionaires can enjoy all that this wonderful life has to offer.

Although *The Healthy Millionaire™* is written for aspiring and successful millionaires, it applies to people of any financial status. The detoxification information can be applied to anyone – from all walks of life. To some, being healthy is itself worth millions, whether or not they aspire to become monetary millionaires.

I am writing from a very personal perspective based on my experiences. All naturopathic doctors practise very differently, and many do not concentrate on the mind, body and spirit connection as I do. Some naturopaths strictly deal with healing the physical body, so the patient feels better. They may have improvements in their physical well-being, but the emotional ailments remain. If the emotional and spiritual issues are not dealt with, the body manifests the same or new symptoms to signal that healing has not yet occurred on all levels.

I have practised naturopathic medicine since 1998, and energetic healing since 1994. My practice focuses on the spirit/mind/body connection and detoxification. I have lectured and taught in the private and corporate sectors about detoxification, and energy healing.

My quest to help others was fuelled by my mother's passing due to cancer in 1991. When my mother could not be helped by conventional medicine, I believe she felt best when she followed the information in the book *How to Get Well*, written by the naturopathic doctor Paavo Airola. I also began reading the information, and friends in high school would call me up when they were sick and ask for my "naturopathic advice," even though I didn't know at the time I would go on to become a naturopathic doctor. I was also heavily influenced by my father, a psychotherapist who dealt with clients in the mental/emotional sphere. I began to realize at a young age that if you didn't feel well emotionally, you didn't feel well physically. Naturopathy was the only profession I knew of that addressed emotional health, alongside that of the physical body.

At the end of my first year at naturopathic college, I was trained in craniosacral therapy. I was beginning to "see" things beyond the physical, as I worked on classmates, friends, and family members. My intuition and gut feelings had always been good before that, but learning about craniosacral therapy really helped me to open my third eye. I became super-intuitive over the next three years while at naturopathic college. This was a safe environment in which to explore "seeing" abilities, because many of my classmates were developing spiritually at the same rate as I was. The real test for me was when I graduated and went into the real world. I had a fear of sharing my true intuitions with my patients. I stopped "reading" people for about a year. Then a former classmate came to see me and asked if I was still doing my "energetic stuff." When I told her no, she was shocked. It was a lesson for me, and I started again that same day. I haven't stopped since.

Some people say I have a gift to be able to practise and "see" what I do. I believe we are all gifted in the same ways that I may be. I have chosen to develop this talent with lots and lots of practise. I have also worked on cleansing and detoxifying my own "stuff," to be a clearer channel for others. I am by no means perfect. And if you see me at Starbucks with a coffee, it is because I try to enjoy life and not get too uptight about living a totally naturopathic life. My patients are sometimes shocked that I do not eat all organic foods, and I am not a vegetarian. I try to follow what I have written in this book about eighty per cent of the time. A girl still needs her chocolate and coffee, once in a while!

Writing books is my contribution to reaching a larger group of people. Global change evolves when we change ourselves, bit by bit, day by day. Our energy then changes, which then automatically changes the energies of those around us. I hope you are able to implement at least one idea learned from this book, and, above all else, enjoy the life you are meant to live!

Dr. Janine Bowring, ND

ACKNOWLEDGEMENTS

Thank you to God, you make it all possible. My heartfelt thanks to my husband, whose encouragement helped me to finish this project when I didn't know how or where I would get the energy to do it. To my children, who were patient enough and slept at least an hour during the afternoon so I could get to the computer to write. Thanks to my dad and brother, for their wisdom over the years. Thank you to my patients, who have taught me more collectively about healing and how the body, mind and spirit work together than I could have ever learned in school. Thank you to Dolce Book Publishing Inc. for bringing this project to life. Thank you to Josie for her kind advice, and to Liz for her contributions and friendship. Debbie, thank you for helping me get this book finished the first time. Thank you Virginia, for your help and keeping me healthy throughout this process.

AN INTRODUCTION: THE SECRET TO MANIFESTING HEALTH AND WEALTH

Toxins

A toxin can be described as: "A poisonous substance, especially a protein that is produced by living cells or organisms, and is capable of causing disease when introduced into the body tissues, but is often also capable of inducing and neutralizing antibodies or antitoxins."[1]

My definition of a toxin differs slightly. I define a toxin as any substance, be it in physical, emotional or spiritual form, which has either a positive or negative effect on the host. I include the realms beyond the physical, because emotions and energetic imbalances can be toxic to our systems and are often the root cause of disease.

When considering the overall health of an individual, toxins can be good, or not so good.

Good Toxins

There are only a few toxins that could be considered positive. I consider emotional toxins, such as anger or guilt, to be positive, only if they force one to become more aware of his or her situation, and perhaps change behaviours. Emotional toxins, if held for a reasonable period of time, are usually the impetus for change, ultimately improving the health of an individual. Physical toxins can be positive if they induce a detoxification process that allows the physical body to heal. For example, if someone with chronic constipation and headaches contracts food poisoning and develops vomiting and diarrhea for three days, they may end up feeling much better afterward. Why? Because the toxin (the bacteria that caused the food poisoning) acted as an agent to purge everything out of the system. The overall toxic load was lessened and the individual feels better – after living next to a toilet for three days. I believe everything happens for a reason. The next time you get sick, see it as a detoxification process that was meant to happen anyway.

Bad Toxins

Most toxins can be considered undesirable, because they impede the body's natural ability to function. The body is intelligent and tries to eliminate toxins through the major emunctories, or eliminative organs, including the liver, lungs, digestive tract, skin, and kidneys. These organs are the most important in keeping us alive – even without any exposure to toxins. The truth is: We are all exposed. From conception to death, our bodies are always struggling to defend themselves and conquer toxins. Today, babies are born toxic. The accumulative nature of toxins (called bioaccumulation) in the human body means that toxins are passed from mother to child in utero. Breast milk, which was once the most pure food source, is now contaminated in all women with pesticide residues, heavy metals and numerous other chemicals that are deleterious to the newborn's health.

Industrial Revolution

The industrial revolution has scarred the health of man. The influx of toxins from industry, pesticides, insecticides, herbicides, transportation, and modern life conveniences has contributed to today's high incidence of disease due to toxicity. There are few diseases that exist without some link to toxicity. Naturopathic medicine addresses toxicity as a cause for disease, whereas allopathic medicine (conventional medicine) often contributes to the toxic load with pharmaceuticals.

Source of Toxins

Toxins enter our bodies from a variety of sources. The most common toxins we encounter on a daily basis are automobile exhaust fumes, pesticides, and insecticides on our food and toxins in the local water supply. We also add to our toxic load with the chemicals we use to clean our homes, in personal hygiene products, such as soap and shampoo, and in the medicines we take. Most of us are unaware of the amount of toxins we inhale, absorb through the skin and ingest on a daily basis. Awareness of these sources of toxins helps to guide us to healthier choices. Whenever I lecture about toxicity and disease, I always remind my listeners that many toxins we do not have a choice over, such as the ones that were passed down from our mothers when we were in the womb, or from mercury amalgams that were placed in our mouths as children. However, there are many toxins that are consciously avoidable in our food supply, cleaning solutions, and beauty products.

Pharmaceutical Drugs

The next time your doctor prescribes you a pharmaceutical drug, ask him or her to read you the list of ingredients and their effects on the liver, kidneys and digestive tract. The truth is that most pharmaceutical drugs have a toxic effect on these organs. Modern medicine is very good at the quick fix. Your cholesterol is high and you take a drug and within a couple weeks, if that, it is normal again. You are healed, right? Well, not really. The question to ask is why was your cholesterol high in the first place? Instead of putting a band-aid (the drug) on the symptom, it makes more sense to treat the underlying cause of the cholesterol issue – usually stemming from toxicity. The cholesterol-lowering drug has a whole host of toxicity-related issues that can be harmful, and it can cause a list of symptoms on its own.

Heavy Metal Toxicity
Heavy metal toxicity is currently a growing concern in health care. The most abundant source of direct heavy metal exposure is in the mouth, from silver dental amalgams or fillings. Other sources of heavy metal exposure include food, water, building supplies, personal hygiene products, cosmetics – the list goes on and on. It is almost impossible for us to eat, drink, live or clean ourselves anymore without being exposed to these toxins. Thankfully, there are ways to detoxify these harmful substances. Our exposure isn't so much the problem anymore. We are all continuously exposed. The key is the way we eliminate these toxins – in the most effective, timely and safest manner.

Electromagnetic Fields
Electromagnetic fields (EMFs) are a hidden source of toxicity that most of us encounter. Today's aspiring or accomplished millionaire most likely works on or around modern conveniences, such as cell phones, computers, and handheld electronic devices. Other sources of EMFs include overhead electrical high-power lines, microwave ovens and all electronics that are plugged into the wall. The problem with these fields of energy is that they disrupt the normal electromagnetic spin of the cells in our bodies, and can have negative consequences on our health. I do not believe that we should avoid the use of such necessary tools in business, however, whenever possible, we should limit exposure.

Where Toxins Reside
Physical toxins reside in most, if not all, of the internal organs. The body naturally tries to eliminate the toxins through the major emunctories, or eliminative organs – the lungs, kidneys, liver, digestive tract and skin. For this reason, these organs are usually the primary sources of toxin accumulation.

Emotional Toxins
Emotional toxins that are not effectively dealt with remain in the conscious or subconscious mind. These toxins can be potentially more threatening to the health of the overall body, as they can fester and cause the physical body to slowly break down. Unhealthy emotions such as anger, resentment,

guilt, sadness and jealousy, are all toxic if retained for too long. Most, if not all, cancer patients I have treated have had emotions that were not cleared from years ago. Emotional trauma that is not effectively treated can be the difference between health and disease.

Spiritual Toxins

Spiritual toxicity is more common than we think. Whenever our spirit is not fulfilled, or we are not fulfilling our soul's purpose, we are accumulating spiritual toxicity. Spiritual toxicity is directly related to the way our physical body looks, feels, and functions. People usually look and feel their best when they are truly happy and enjoying life. If you look at someone who has just fallen in love, they are radiant. Love is a true spiritual fulfilment, and the physical body changes when love is felt in every cell. This is what we were all meant to experience, every moment of each day on Earth. Anything other than love is toxic to our spirit, and needs to be detoxified.

The Detoxification Process

Cleaning the physical, emotional and spiritual toxins from our systems can be a lifelong process. *The Healthy Millionaire*™ provides easy-to-follow guidelines to remove toxins from the internal organs of excretion, the mind, and most importantly, the spirit.

Definition of Naturopathy

Naturopathy combines the art and science of diagnosis, and treatment of the body's imbalances or illnesses with the use of non-invasive, natural healing modalities (acupuncture, supplementation, herbal medicine, homeopathy, and lifestyle counselling). Naturopathic doctors believe that the body has an inherent ability to heal itself. With the use of natural supplements and treatments, a naturopath helps the patient regain health and balance in the body, mind and spirit.

Principles of Naturopathic Medicine

There are six principles of naturopathic medicine that all naturopathic doctors follow:

1) Tolle Causam – **treat the cause** of disease. I like to use the analogy of a dandelion. If you want to get rid of the weed, you need to dig deep into the ground and remove the whole root. If you merely cut off the leaves, the root remains, and the dandelion will grow back in no time. The same is true with disease. You need to treat the root cause and not just the symptoms. Symptomatic relief can act as a band-aid on the

underlying problem. If the root cause of disease is alleviated, there is no need for the symptoms to stick around.

2) Primum non Nocere – **first do no harm**
Naturopathic doctors use gentle techniques and remedies to allow the body to heal itself. For the most part, our treatments are non-invasive.

3) Docere – **doctor as teacher**
The naturopath acts as a teacher to the patient, and helps them to understand their own body's wisdom.

4) Vis Medicatrix Naturae – **support the healing power of nature**
Nature provides many healing qualities, which are harnessed by the naturopath and put into practical use for the patient.

5) Treat the Whole Person
The naturopathic physician sees the patient as a whole, and treats accordingly. The symptoms are merely one aspect of what is going on internally to cause disease. Every symptom is important to the naturopathic doctor – from what side you sleep on, to the foods you crave. Symptoms in the body are often connected to each other, even if seemingly unrelated. For instance, the digestive system is connected to the skin, and the skin is connected to the lungs. A toxic gastrointestinal (GI) tract can be manifested in acne on the skin. To treat the whole person, both the skin and GI tract need to be addressed in the treatment protocol set out by the naturopath.

6) Prevention
Prevention of disease is key in any situation, and is taken very seriously by naturopathic practitioners. Serious and chronic disease usually manifests in a series of steps, as one becomes more and more toxic. Symptoms that may seem unimportant to an untrained individual may be an indication of impending disease. If treated early enough, the toxicity can be reversed, preventing disease. For example, someone with skin tags and the inability to go for three hours without food before feeling faint may have early signs of diabetes. If the blood sugar and pancreatic issues are addressed early enough, this person need not develop diabetes.

Education
Most naturopaths like to consider themselves as complementary health-care practitioners. Naturopathic doctors complement allopathic

medicine in a non-invasive and practical way, with an emphasis on prevention. Naturopaths can diagnose and treat disease, however, the prescriptions are usually from a natural source, rather than a pharmaceutical drug. Most naturopaths believe that there is a need for an allopathic presence in health care, and hope to bridge the gap between the two different, yet complementary forms of diagnosis and treatment of disease. Unfortunately, some allopathic practitioners still believe in the "quack" labelling of natural practitioners, but with time their views will change because, quite simply, people are getting better with natural remedies.

Naturopathic doctors are licensed practitioners of complementary health care, and have the most complete and comprehensive education of all alternative health professions.

Modalities

The modalities that a naturopathic doctor may use include homeopathy, traditional Chinese medicine, acupuncture, Asian and Western herbal medicine, hydrotherapy, supplementation, dietary counselling, naturopathic manipulation and lifestyle counselling.

Homeopathy

Homeopathy is the medicine in which like cures like. It is based on the law of similars, in which the symptoms induced by taking a remedy in its full strength or mother tincture will produce certain symptoms that will be alleviated when taken in a very diluted dose, otherwise known as a homeopathic remedy. A good example of how homeopathic prescribing works is coffee. Most people would have a difficult time falling asleep if they drank coffee just before bed. However, for someone suffering with insomnia, the homeopathic remedy of coffee, called coffea, would help him or her to sleep. Homeopathy is wonderful because it includes physical, mental and emotional symptoms. One's personality, dreams, fears and phobias are all part of the homeopathic picture that makes up one's constitutional remedy. Homeopathics can also be prescribed for acute conditions such as a headache or the common cold. Homeopathy is used extensively throughout the world, particularly in India, Europe and Australia.

Traditional Chinese Medicine

Traditional Chinese medicine (TCM) is based on the belief that the body has an energy system or chi (qi) that is connected to the five elements: Fire, wood, earth, metal and water. Chi flows along meridians in the body and collects in certain areas or points, known as the acupuncture points. Disease is thought to be sick chi that does not flow properly. The flow of chi can be restored or balanced with the use of Chinese herbs, dietary changes, and acupuncture.

Acupuncture

Acupuncture uses very fine needles in acupuncture points to stimulate chi, or one's vital energy. Acupuncture is also an effective way to detoxify the major organs. Chi is the energy that flows throughout the body and is concentrated in locations known as the acupuncture points. The major internal organs have meridians, or channels that connect a group of acupuncture points. Each organ can then be affected by stimulating these points either with acupuncture needles, or acupressure. The points may be far away from the organ being helped, so, to the layperson, acupuncture may not make a lot of sense. It is very important to obtain a proper Chinese or Asian medical diagnosis from your practitioner before they start acupuncture, because the points are so intricately connected to the internal organs.

Chi is bipolar in nature. It is influenced by yin and yang in the body (Yin can be defined as negative, dark, passive, cold, wet, and feminine, whereas yang is positive, bright, active, dry, hot, and masculine). Either an excess or deficiency of chi in the body causes illness. The absence of chi is death. Acupuncture is helpful at restoring the balance of yin and yang in the channels and organs by manipulating the chi at the acupuncture points. Acupuncture is usually not painful, as many fear it to be.

Pregnancy is usually a contraindication for acupuncture because certain points can stimulate the uterus to contract, causing a miscarriage.

Asian herbal medicine

Eastern herbal medicine includes the use of herbs and traditional formulas used for thousands of years in Asian cultures. The herbs are readily available in North America, and are usually purchased in dried form. These dried herbs are boiled in water and drunk as teas, generally twice a day. Some Chinese patent formulas are dried herbs made into little balls and sold in bottles of pre-made formulas. The dried herbs that are mixed by a practitioner are stronger, and work more quickly than the Chinese patents. The other advantage of these dried herbal formulas is that they are made specifically for your constitution and balance (or imbalance) of yin and yang by the practitioner.

Western herbal medicine

Western herbs are those native to the Western hemisphere, usually North and South America. Common Western herbs include dandelion, echinacea, and milk thistle. Western herbs are prescribed based on symptoms of a patient, and are usually combined by herbalists to have a synergistic effect. Western herbs can be taken as teas, tinctures, tablets, or in capsule form. It is best to buy herbs with the standardized quantity of active ingredients listed on the product to ensure quality. Again, herbal medicines can be harmful, and should be prescribed by a qualified practitioner. Herbal remedies also have interactions with pharmaceutical drugs, and it is potentially dangerous to mix herbs with allopathic drugs. Naturopaths are trained to distinguish which combinations are safe.

Hydrotherapy

Hydrotherapy is the therapeutic use of water. Hydrotherapy uses water at different temperatures to have various effects. For instance, hot water helps to dilate blood vessels and increase circulation, whereas cold water constricts blood vessels and moves blood away from the cooled part. When both hot and cold water are alternately used, it causes a flushing action of the blood, a constriction followed by a dilation, which increases detoxification and blood and lymph flow.

Supplementation

Naturopathic doctors prescribe supplements as required by patients, according to their individual needs. Many vitamins work together with other vitamins and minerals, or compete for absorption with others. This is, again, another reason to be guided by a naturopath or qualified professional when taking vitamins: to ensure that you are not becoming deficient in some vitamins, while perhaps overdosing in others.

Dietary Counselling

Your diet is the foundation of your health and provides the necessary nutrients to sustain life. Naturopaths are trained to study diets and make suggestions to balance nutrient consumption and to optimize absorption and utilization.

Naturopathic manipulation

Naturopathic doctors are trained by chiropractors to perform manipulations to the spine and limbs as required. Although many naturopathic doctors do not choose to do manipulations in their practice, it can be a very useful modality when the need arises. The crack that you hear during a manipulation is merely a gaseous exchange in the joint and not – as is commonly thought and feared – the bones cracking.

Lifestyle counselling

Naturopaths counsel many of their patients on lifestyle habits, such as sleep patterns, stimulant use, and relationship issues. Our lifestyles have much to do with our physical, emotional and spiritual health. Guidance in this area can help to bring balance to the body, mind and spirit.

These are the basic modalities taught at the naturopathic colleges. Individual naturopaths may have extra training in other modalities as well. For instance, craniosacral therapy and homeopathic drainage are modalities that I use frequently in my practice that I learned outside the College of Naturopathic Medicine.

Probably the most commonly asked question in naturopathy is: "What is the difference between naturopathy and homeopathy?" Naturopathy is like the umbrella profession that encompasses many modalities (as listed above), of which homeopathy is one. The training for homeopathy and naturopathy differs tremendously as well. If you are looking for either of these practitioners, be sure to ask for their licence registration number and years of study.

When you visit a naturopathic doctor, the experience is usually very different from that of an allopathic practitioner. The first visit with a naturopath is usually an hour or more in length. In this time, you will be asked numerous questions about your entire body – from your digestion to skin problems, to how often you urinate. The naturopath may also ask personal questions about your home life, work and mental/emotional health. The whole purpose of such a detailed history is to ascertain the root causes of disease. A naturopath looks at the body as a whole, including the mental and spiritual sphere. Everything in the body and mind is connected. If the emotional sphere is not investigated, there is a whole piece of the puzzle that is missing in terms of one's ailments.

Detoxification Definition

What I have come to understand is that practically every known disease arises from some level of toxicity – be it from a physical, mental/ emotional, or spiritual cause. Toxicity and detoxification are popular subjects among naturopathic doctors and complementary health care practitioners, but alarmingly disregarded by the general public and conventional medicine. People still want the quick fix for their ailments and usually do not understand the root cause of their problem, which is generally toxicity.

Detoxification is the process by which the eliminative organs of the body are actively promoted to do their job more efficiently. As mentioned before, the main organs of excretion and detoxification are the lungs, liver, gastrointestinal tract, kidneys and skin.

Toxicity Linked to Cause of Disease

Most diseases are caused by toxicity, be it physical, emotional or spiritual. When toxins are not effectively removed and excreted from the body, they linger and can disrupt the chemistry of the internal environment of the cells. For example, if you get a splinter in your hand and do not remove it promptly, the body will attempt to drive it out. The area around the splinter will become inflamed, and the immune system will be activated because an invader has entered the system. White blood cells will act to clear up the debris caused by the splinter. In time, pus will form and the splinter will come out as an eruption, or will dissolve altogether. The skin will heal as if nothing ever happened.

However, if the immune system is weak, these normal processes may not happen effectively. This may lead to a more serious infection, involving the lymph nodes and causing more disruption of the entire organism. If this is true for a tiny splinter, think how our bodies may not be up to the challenge when under prolonged stress. Stress depletes our immune systems, and when faced with more serious toxins, our bodies are not always able to clear them out, which leads to disease.

When you experience symptoms of any kind in your body, it is an indication that something has gone wrong. I call symptoms "red flags," which indicate a disruption in the normal functioning of the body, mind or spirit. Unfortunately, we often overlook or ignore symptoms for a long time before we have them checked out by a doctor. Many of us have a fear of developing a disease that keeps us in denial about our symptoms. Others are so out of touch with their bodies that they literally need to be knocked over the head or in a car accident to force them to take a look at their health. The other extreme includes those who are hypochondriacal, and regard every twinge or pain in their bodies as a disease of some sort.

What I regard as a real symptom is something that occurs frequently and repeats in quality of discomfort or peculiarity. For instance, a twinge of pain felt once in the right temple for two seconds, which is not due to a blow in the head or another cause, would not be a symptom. But a recurring headache over the right temple that happens when someone is hungry and hasn't eaten for four hours would be a symptom.

A naturopathic doctor regards symptoms differently than other medical professionals. A naturopath gives weight to all symptoms, no matter how remote or unrelated they may seem. Naturopaths who practise homeopathy ask their patients weird and wonderful questions ranging from, "What position do you sleep in?" to, "What are your fears or phobias?" All symptoms in homeopathy form a picture. The goal of the homeopathic prescriber is to match the patient's symptoms as closely as possible to that of the remedies.

"Dis-ease" means a lack of ease in the body. We should avoid labelling and judging people based on the disease with which they have been diagnosed. It is so easy-even for patients-to label themselves as "a cancer patient" or "an arthritis sufferer."

However, allopathic medical classifications of disease are necessary to group similar toxicity patterns in individuals in order to treat them with the correct drugs or protocols. Naturopathic medicine differs somewhat from this, in that naturopathic doctors treat patients as individuals with a variety of symptoms of toxicity, rather than people with diseases. I can have ten patients who have all been diagnosed with polycystic ovaries, yet their symptoms, manifestation of the toxicity, and my treatment protocol will differ for each woman.

In practice, I have noted patterns of personality traits that match other patients with the same disease process. There are always some exceptions, but for the most part, the mental picture of some types of diseases is strikingly similar. For example, I notice a pattern in all cancer patients that somewhere in their psyche, they believe that they should take care of others before they take care of themselves. Cancer patients often have many fears, and fear cancer long before they develop it.

Only thirty per cent of disease manifestation is due to genetics. This means that the remaining seventy per cent must be from other factors. Most of these relate to diet, lifestyle, mental/emotional and spiritual health. Many diseases are passed down the family tree because the family mind-set or emotional baggage is also passed down, as well as dietary and lifestyle habits. The best thing you can do for yourself and your health is to be the black sheep of the family. This means eating differently, and living a more healthful lifestyle with less exposure to toxins. Most importantly, it is essential to your health to let go of the emotional patterns that repeat in your family. If you think like your parents do, it is quite likely you will develop the same problems they did. I also believe that you are more likely to manifest a disease if you know it well enough, and have learned all about its symptoms from seeing its effects on a loved one. It's as if the disease or ailment leaves an imprint in your being or energy field that can be manifested at any time.

Pharmaceutical Drugs and Toxicity

Unfortunately, the wide use of pharmaceutical drugs has increased our overall toxicity massively. I have witnessed the snowball effect caused by drugs, as patients need more drugs to alleviate symptoms caused by the chemicals in the first place.

Most, if not all, pharmaceutical drugs need to be detoxified by the major emunctories. Usually, the liver and kidneys are the organs responsible for their breakdown and elimination. With prolonged exposure to these drugs, the toxicity in these organs increases, which causes new symptoms that need to be alleviated by further drugs.

A good example of this cascade of events is the use of the birth control pill (BCP). BCPs are given to women to regulate their periods and decrease cramping. The root cause of cramping and irregular periods is usually liver toxicity. The BCP may improve the symptoms associated with the periods, but it also increases liver toxicity. When the woman goes off the pill, her liver toxicity is worse than when she started, and her symptoms will often reflect this change. Occasionally, it takes months to get the period back because it was suppressed by the synthetic hormones in the pills.

CHAPTER 1 | DETOXIFICATION OF THE BODY

Detoxification has been practised since the early days of humankind as a spiritual and physical cleansing of the body, mind and spirit. Due to the toxic burden our bodies encounter every day in the food we eat – the air we breathe and the water we drink and in which we bathe – we need to cleanse regularly. Detoxification of the physical body is imperative, especially if we are sick in any way. Toxins accumulate and can lead to ill health if they are not addressed. Toxins either come from outside the body (exogenous), or are produced inside the body (endogenous). Exogenous toxins include chemicals, pesticides, insecticides, toxic gases and mould. Endogenous toxins are produced inside the body from protein breakdown and from substances produced by bacteria, yeast and fungi in the digestive tract.

Physical detoxification involves the removal of toxins from the internal organs of excretion in which they may be stored, and improving the function of these organs, so that they are more efficient in their detoxification processes.

Opening the Organs of Excretion

Emunctories are eliminative organs. They process and eliminate toxins from the body. They act as filters to remove the waste that is no longer needed. When the emunctories are working well, an individual is usually healthy; when they are not working well, disease sets in. Some authorities on detoxification indicate that all disease stems from toxicity and the inability of one (or a combination) of these organs to work efficiently. The five major emunctories are the liver, lungs, skin, gastrointestinal tract and kidneys.

Function of the Liver

The liver filters approximately one litre of blood each minute. The liver has three main functions:

1) Vascular filtration of blood
2) Metabolism
3) Secretion and excretion of bile that flows through the bile ducts and into the digestive tract for the breakdown of fats.

The liver is remarkable in that it can lose up to seventy per cent of its capability and still not be diagnostically detected for liver disease. The liver has the ability to regenerate on its own, if it is free from toxic exposure. It is an organ that acts as a reservoir for blood and can deliver it to the body if needed. The liver is also responsible for approximately half of the body's lymph formation. Blood that comes from the intestines, which is usually full of bacteria, passes through the liver and Kupffer cells. The Kupffer cells are macrophages – the Pac-Mans of the immune system. They eat up and digest bacteria on contact. The blood is purified by the liver's Kupffer cells, and few bacteria make it into the systemic circulation for this reason.[2]

The liver has two phases of detoxification: Phase 1 and Phase 2 detoxification. Phase 1 involves either direct neutralization of the toxin, or bio-transformation (modification) of the toxin to be eliminated by Phase 2 enzymes. Bio-transformation can be potentially harmful if the Phase 2 enzymes are not efficient enough at clearing the metabolites (the breakdown products of metabolism). These metabolites are often more toxic after Phase 1 than the original toxin. Phase 1 detoxification uses a class of enzymes called cytochrome P450.

Phase 2 involves the attachment of chemical groups to the toxin, which either neutralizes it, or makes it easier for it to be excreted by the kidneys or in the bile. Phase 2 enzymes can work on some toxins directly, but others must first be bio-transformed in Phase 1.

The liver and the kidneys are the major detoxifiers of pharmaceutical drugs. Almost every drug needs to be cleared through the liver and kidneys. This is why so many side effects of drugs are actually liver symptoms. For this reason, it is best to avoid drugs whenever possible, because they only add to the toxicity of the liver, thereby, making the underlying condition worse – even if the symptoms are suppressed. The symptoms of liver toxicity are very common and often seemingly unrelated to the liver. These are some of the most common signs and symptoms of liver toxicity:

- Nausea
- Fatigue
- Overweight
- Abdominal bloating
- Premenstrual syndrome (PMS)
- Menstrual irregularities and pain
- Poor digestion
- Headaches, migraines, tension headaches
- Sore neck and trapezius muscles
- Skin diseases, eczema, psoriasis

How to Detoxify the Liver

The simplest way to detoxify the liver is to consume large amounts of dark green, leafy vegetables. The more bitter the better, according to Chinese medicine. These foods contain many of the nutrients required for the Phase 1 and 2 enzyme systems, and the bitter taste stimulates the liver and gallbladder to produce and secrete bile for digestion. I usually suggest that a person eats six cups of raw greens a day. They usually look at me as if I'm crazy, until I explain that if you steam six cups of raw greens, they usually shrink down to half the size.

Squeezing some fresh lemon in water and drinking it throughout the day is another way to detoxify the liver. Lemons contain d-limonene, and mormolin, which are compounds that induce Phase 2 detoxification in the liver, specifically glucuronidation and glutathione conjugation. Use 1/4 to 1/2 a lemon in 8 oz. of water. Warm water is better at stimulating the digestive process and moving the bowels. Many of my patients find that it is easier to drink their eight glasses of water a day if there is lemon to jazz it up a little. Please note that for some, the lemon may be too acidic for the teeth, which can cause sensitivity or breakdown of the enamel. For sensitive individuals, only use the lemon in water once a day at a higher concentration, and then brush the teeth soon after.

Milk thistle *(Silybum marianum)* is probably the most commonly used Western herb for liver detoxification. This herb has the dual effect of liver protection and regeneration, as well as detoxification. The seeds of the plant are used medicinally. Milk thistle acts as a cholagogue, which is an agent that increases bile flow from the gallbladder and liver, it increases lactation in nursing women, and it is a demulcent, a soothing herb for the digestive tract. Milk thistle increases detoxification of cells by increasing cellular respiration, increasing glutathione and acts as an antioxidant.[3] Active ingredients: Silybin, silydianin, silychristine.[4]
Milk Thistle is commonly used in detoxification formulas. It is best used as a standardized extract of seventy per cent silymarin. See my formulation Vita Detox™ from VitaTree™ Nutritionals at www.vitatree.ca.

Castor oil packs can be used to detoxify the liver. They were a commonly used tool by Edgar Cayce, a healer and medical intuitive who gave patients "readings" based on information he channelled. To make a castor oil pack, soak an unbleached cotton or flannel piece of fabric about one square foot with cold-pressed castor oil. (Organic, hexane-free castor oil is best). Wring out excess castor oil, so the cloth is soaked, but not dripping. Place the castor oil-filled cloth over your liver, which is located under your right rib cage. Cover the pack with plastic wrap. And cover the plastic with an old towel, followed by a hot water bottle. Do not use a heating pad because the electromagnetic energy emitted is not healthy. Leave in place for forty-five to ninety minutes. This can be done two to three times a week. The castor oil pack can be re-used by the same person. Store in a covered glass container.

In homeopathy, Chelidonium is a commonly used remedy to clear the liver of toxins. Chelidonium is indicated for someone with[5 6]:

- Complaints on the right side of the body
- May be sad or anxious
- Irritability
- Pain in the liver and gallbladder area
- Skin tinted yellow from jaundice
- Pain that moves from the liver to the right shoulder
- Loose stools that float and are yellow
- Feels better drinking hot milk
- Craves dairy products, warm drinks

Homeopathic Chelidonium (not to be confused with herbal chelidonium, which can be toxic at high doses), can be found either alone in a 6,30 or 200 potency. Generally, the lower the potency or dilutions, the more of a physiological effect the remedy will have, and the higher potencies tend to work more on the psychological realm.

There are many other remedies for clearing the liver. Your naturopathic doctor, who is trained to diagnose and monitor liver health, should be the one to prescribe these remedies.

Function of the Lungs

The function of the lungs is to inhale oxygen, which will be used for fuel in the body. They also serve a protective function against airborne pathogens, such as dust, pollen, bacteria, fungal spores and viruses. The lungs have several features that help to protect themselves from these invaders.

- There are sensory endings in the nasal passages, trachea and bronchi that cause sneezing and coughing reflexes to occur if irritated.
- Larger particles are trapped in nose hairs and in the nasal passage.

(This is why one should breathe through the nose, rather than the mouth, especially if in contact with airborne pathogens).
- Small hair-like projections are on the lung cells that propel inhaled particles to the trachea, so that they can be coughed up or swallowed.
- Mucous secreted by lung cells traps particles.

The mechanism of breathing involves movement of the diaphragm, a large muscle that extends across the entire body at the level of the lower rib cage. The muscles between the ribs also help in breathing. These are the intercostal muscles. When we inhale, the diaphragm contracts and pulls the lower surfaces of the lungs down and air rushes in. The ribs lift during inhalation from the contraction of the intercostal muscles. When we exhale, the diaphragm relaxes and the elastic recoil of the lungs, the chest wall, and the abdominal structures compress or squeeze the air out of the lungs.

Symptoms of lung toxicity are as follows:
- Cough – dry and/or mucous-producing
- Asthma
- Allergies
- Wheezing
- Skin eruptions*

* In Chinese medicine, the lungs are related to the skin. Sometimes, toxicity in the lungs that cannot escape via the lungs comes out on the skin in the form of a rash or eruption.

How to Detoxify the Lungs

Many of the millionaires that I have interviewed as patients are smokers. I believe that once someone has become financially successful, they may adopt an attitude of being invincible, whether it is with finances or their health. Smoking is also a social activity, and those who want to quit find it difficult to when the people around them smoke. Smoking, as we all know, is a destructive and addictive practice. Smoking definitely places a large burden on the lungs and forces them to detoxify the chemicals and pesticides found in cigarettes. Even second-hand smoke is a concern, in regards to lung toxicity.

Lung detoxification can be accomplished by deep-breathing exercises. For people with chronic lung toxicity, I recommend spending as much time as possible in fresh air. For some people – especially children with asthma – this means getting out of the big city and going to the country on the weekends, or whenever possible. Exercises, such as yoga and Pilates, can train the diaphragm and intercostal muscles to expand the lungs and compress the stale air from the lungs. This increased perfusion of fresh air into the lungs helps to clear them of toxic residues. And if you do smoke, stop!

There are some essential oils that are very effective in helping to clear the lungs of toxins. When the following oils are inhaled deeply, they can have a profound effect. Use two to three drops on a damp cloth and inhale deeply as needed, or place one to two drops of each in a pot of boiled water, cover your head with a towel and inhale the steam for fifteen to twenty minutes.

OIL	THERAPEUTIC EFFECT
Eucalyptus	Anti-inflammatory, antiseptic, antibiotic, diuretic, analgesic, antiviral
Tea tree	Antibacterial, antiviral, antifungal
Hyssop	Antibacterial, antiviral, improves circulation, calms nerves
Thyme	Antibacterial, antiviral, improves immunity
Pine	Antibacterial, antiviral, for any respiratory or chest problem[7]

Herbal medicine for the lungs

The following herbs can be used for clearing mucous and toxins in the lungs and for soothing a cough:

Coltsfoot – expectorant, anti-tussive, anti-spasmodic, anti-catarrhal, demulcent
Mullein – expectorant, demulcent, anti-inflammatory, anti-spasmodic
White Horehound – expectorant, anti-spasmodic
Licorice – expectorant, demulcent, anti-spasmodic
Lobelia – anti-asthmatic, anti-spasmodic, expectorant
Borage – expectorant, anti-inflammatory
Cayenne – stimulant, anti-catarrhal, anti-microbial[8]

Definitions of herbal properties:

Expectorant: Helps to bring up mucous to rid it from the body

Anti-tussive: Stops coughing
Anti-spasmodic: Stops spasms in the lungs
Anti-catarrhal: Stops mucous from forming
Demulcent: Soothing to mucous membranes
These herbs are contraindicated in pregnancy, lactation, hypertension, cardiovascular disease, thyroid disease, diabetes, or for men with difficulty urinating due to an enlarged prostate.

Homeopathic remedies for the lungs

Antimonium tartaricum
Stubborn loose cough
Rattling in chest
Not much expectoration
Infants with bronchitis with the above symptoms
Very sleepy with cough
Irritable
Vomiting with cough, may be nauseated

Spongia tosta
Dry, barking cough
Croupy cough, sounds like a "seal bark"
Cough starts from a tickling in the throat
Cough improves with drinking

Rumex crispus
Cough from cold air causing a tickle in the throat
Cough better from drinking
Cough from laughing, talking
Cough worse from taking clothes off, uncovering

Phosphorus
Colds go straight to the chest with a cough when they get sick
Cough lingers
Cough worse laying on left side of body, better on the right
Cough from tickle in the throat
Cough is worse in the cold air
Thirst for ice cold drinks[9]

The standard dosage is prescribed best by your naturopathic doctor or health care professional.

Function of the Skin

The skin is the largest organ of the body. Most of what you put on the skin is absorbed into the body. The skin is also a dumping ground for internal organ toxicity. When the internal organs become overwhelmed by accumulated toxins, they often resort to dumping these chemicals, which end up manifesting in skin symptoms. Almost any rash can be seen as a detoxification reaction to either an internal or external toxin. From Herring's Law, a toxin will work its way out of the body from inside to out. For this reason, most skin reactions are detoxification. It is one of the body's inherent red flag signals that tell us a detoxification process is occurring.

The skin has an enzyme system, called cytochrome p450, which converts toxins into another form that is more easily metabolized and excreted. The skin also converts fat-soluble chemicals into more water-soluble forms for excretion. For this reason, perspiration is one of the few ways we can eliminate toxins stored in fat cells.

Any form of skin rash, eruption or irritation is a sign of skin toxicity. When toxins are abundant in the major emunctories and these routes of detoxification are not efficient, the toxins can come to the surface of the body, namely the skin.

How to Detoxify the Skin

Sweating is one of the best ways to detoxify the skin. Exercise that induces a good sweat is not only beneficial for the lungs and heart, but also for general detoxification through the skin. Saunas are also recommended for this purpose. It is also very important to drink a lot of water in order to be able to produce more perspiration. Water also keeps the skin hydrated and younger looking.

Far infrared (FIR) saunas are reported to have better detoxifying effects compared with traditional saunas and steam rooms. FIR is the same as the heat we absorb from the sun, but without the ultraviolet rays that can be damaging to the skin. It is just below red light in the electromagnetic spectrum of light, and cannot be seen, only felt as heat. FIR energy is absorbed by our bodies and penetrates into the fat and muscles of the body – not superficially, as in regular saunas. For this reason, it has a greater ability to detoxify the lymphatic system and fat cells.

FIR saunas are more comfortable because the ambient temperature is not as hot as the traditional sauna. The following is a list of ailments that reportedly benefit from FIR saunas:

- Damaged tissues, such as sprains, strains, muscle pain
- Arthritis
- Acne
- Cellulite
- Upper respiratory tract infections
- Ear infections
- Heavy metal toxicity
- Obesity[10]

FIR saunas increase one's perspiration and metabolic rate. It is possible to burn up to 600 calories in one thirty-minute session in a FIR sauna, and perspire 500 grams of sweat. This type of sauna also increases the heart rate and improves circulation.

Saunas are generally not recommended for pregnant and lactating women, those with auto-immune disorders such as lupus, and severely depleted adrenal function. Always check with your health practitioner before beginning a sauna protocol, and make sure that adequate water is consumed before, during and after a sauna.

I often suggest that my millionaire patients purchase their own FIR sauna for their homes. But not all FIR saunas are created equal. There is a huge variance in quality and strength of penetration from the emitters. Some FIR saunas can be toxic if the wood is imported. Please see www.healthymillionairebook.com for more information on the highest quality FIR saunas.

Wet brushing is effective for detoxifying the skin and improving lymphatic flow. Dry brushing is usually recommended in the literature for the same reason, however, it is too harsh and can damage skin cells. Wet brushing has the same beneficial effects as dry brushing, but the layer of water is protective to the skin. To perform wet brushing, use a natural bristle body brush in the shower. Start with the feet, and brush in clockwise circles towards the top of the legs. The pressure should be enough to cause a slight reddening of the skin, yet not so hard as to cause pain. Continue on the lower abdomen, towards the heart. Then brush the hands and forearms to the shoulders. You always move towards the heart, where the lymph is filtered. Wet brushing improves circulation, lymphatic flow and detoxification, and makes the skin more efficient for detoxification.

Some supplements support skin healing and detoxification (see chart below for an explanation of skin remedies and how they are helpful).

SUPPLEMENT	DOSAGE	FUNCTION
Vitamin E	Use oil externally on closed skin	Protects skin from free radical damage, heals scars
Vitamin A	5,000 IU per day	Heals and rebuilds skin
Evening Primrose Oil	2 - 500 mg capsules; 3 times a day	Heals skin and is anti-inflammatory due to linoleic acid
Tea Tree Oil	Externally as required	Antiseptic, antifungal
Unda 270 Homeopathic Skin Cream (available from a naturopath)	Externally as required	Detoxifies skin cells, heals rashes without suppressing the eruption
Aloe Vera Gel	Externally as required	Heals damaged skin cells
Fish Oils	Taken internally as a supplement with EPA and DHA (See Chapter Two: Diet; Fish) 600 - 1,000 mg pure fish oil per day, with food	Soothes irritations, anti-inflammatory, heals skin eruptions

I usually caution patients about the skincare products that they are using. There are many harmful chemicals in creams, soaps, make-up, shampoos and conditioners that are absorbed through the skin into the bloodstream. Cosmetics and beauty products are a source of hidden toxins that are absorbed into our systems daily. They are a source of preventable toxin exposure and can be minimized when we are educated about their harmful effects and what products we can use as alternatives.

Some of the toxins found in health and beauty products that should be avoided are as follows:

1. Methyl, propyl, butyl, ethyl alcohols

These are used as preservatives in many cosmetics. (Eg. Isopropyl alcohol, or rubbing alcohol, is toxic to the liver).

2. Sodium laurel sulfate

Used in shampoos, soaps and conditioners, this is linked to urinary tract infections, bladder and kidney toxicity, genital disorders, eye irritation, hair loss and allergic reactions.

3. Colour

Usually labelled FD&C Blue, Red, Yellow, and so on, they are derived from coal tar and have been linked to hyperactivity and attention deficit disorder. They are particularly harmful for children who are often sensitive to these ingredients.

4. Triethanolamine (TEA) and Diethanolamine (DEA)

These chemicals are solvents, emulsifiers and detergents that help to adjust the pH in products. They are linked to kidney and liver toxicity.

5. Imidazolidinyl urea, Diazolidinyl urea

Both are preservatives that release formaldehyde in the body. (See formaldehyde toxicity below.[11])

Toxicity from the internal organs is mapped on the face. The face reflects where toxicity lies in the deeper organs and can give clues as to which organs need to be detoxified. Those who have acne breakouts on particular areas of the face can link that toxicity to the internal environment of their system.

For instance, repetitive breakouts on the chin indicate large intestine toxicity, and possible constipation, because the toxins are not being released efficiently. The forehead area reflects health in the digestive tract. The whites of the eyes indicate the health of the liver. If they are red or yellowish, the liver may be congested. If the irises of the eyes contain whitish concentric lines, this indicates chronic stress. The kidneys are reflected in the area beneath the eyes. Puffiness or dark circles under the eyes indicate kidney weakness. The heart is mapped on the nose. Chronic redness on the cheeks indicates stomach problems. Transverse creases on the earlobes indicate heart problems. Many small lines on the lips indicate bowel toxicity. Longitudinal lines on the cheeks indicate issues with the lungs. The reproductive organs are mapped on the lower corners of the mouth as wrinkles.

> Corticosteroid creams (containing cortisone) are suppressive to the detoxification process. These creams make the rash disappear, but in actual fact, drive the toxins back into the body to an internal organ.

Problems with the ileocecal valve, where the small and large intestine join, can be seen at the corners of the mouth.

The most commonly affected internal organs are the lungs. In Chinese medicine, the lungs are related to the skin. If you suppress the toxins from coming out of the skin, they go back inside the body to the lungs. The best example, and unfortunately a common one, is the treatment of eczema in children. They are often given corticosteroid creams to clear up the eczema. Yes, the eczema goes away nicely with the cream, but very often the child will develop asthma within months of the suppression. On a positive note, when treated naturopathically, the child's asthma disappears first and then the eczema returns briefly.

Herring's Law of Healing states that disease will arise from a certain sequence of events. When the disease is cured, the sequence of events will again be followed, but in reverse order. An example is childhood eczema that manifests as an itchy skin rash. If it is suppressed with corticosteroid cream, it may develop into asthma in the lungs. The external disease became internal. If the asthma is treated homeopathically, the asthma will first disappear, followed by another eruption of the eczema. The symptoms go from the interior of the body to the exterior. This follows the laws of homotoxicology, in which there is a definite sequence of events as toxins go deeper into the body, causing more serious disease. When the organs and tissues are detoxified, there may be signs or symptoms that indicate the toxins are reverting and going to a more external part of the body.

Function of Gastrointestinal Tract

The gastrointestinal (GI) tract is a long tube, approximately fifteen feet long. The stomach and small intestine do most of the breakdown of food particles, with the help of digestive enzymes. The large intestine or bowel converts the liquid small intestine contents (chyme) into solid, indigestible waste material. The large intestine then removes water from the chyme and allows its 400 or more species of bacteria to further break down carbohydrates and other nutrients. The bowel also helps to maintain the body's electrolyte balance, and provides immunological defense against micro-organisms such as bacteria, parasites and fungi. The feces are then ready for excretion via the rectum.

Symptoms of gastrointestinal toxicity are:

- Bloating
- Gas
- Diarrhea
- Stomach aches
- Constipation
- Irregular bowel movements
- Less than one bowel movement per day
- Mucous in stool
- Intestinal blood in stool (not from hemorrhoids)
- Fatigue, especially after eating
- Skin eruptions
- Allergies
- Chronic upper respiratory tract infections

Proper elimination of waste is essential for efficient GI detoxification. Ideally, we should have one bowel movement a day for every decent-sized meal. This means at least two bowel movements a day, preferably three. I find it rare for a person eating the Standard American Diet (S.A.D.) to eliminate this frequently. In other countries, it is normal for everyone to evacuate this much. I have heard of an African tribe whose translation for greeting one another was, "How are you pooping today?" instead of, "Hello" or, "How are you?" This goes to show you how important bowel movements are in terms of overall health to this group of people.

On the road to wealth, hectic schedules sometimes impede the normal instincts of elimination. In other words, when you have to go, go. Don't wait to finish typing the email, or sending the fax, and so on.

Dysbiosis and Leaky Gut Syndrome

Dysbiosis is a term used to describe a condition in the GI tract in which an imbalance of good and bad gut bacteria occurs. This is an extremely common phenomenon, and can happen if any of the following scenarios are true in the previous ten to fifteen years for the patient:

- Antibiotic use
- Synthetic hormone use (cortisone, birth control pills, hormone replacement therapy)
- Severe stress
- Parasitic infection of the GI tract

- Bacterial infection of the GI tract
- Vaccination

The GI tract has over 400 species of bacteria colonizing it. Some of these bacteria are beneficial, others are not. The good bacteria include *Lactobacillus acidophilus, Lactobacillus bulgaricus, Lactobacillus casei* and *Bifidobacterium bifidum*. Lactobacilli are the predominant bacteria of the small intestine and Bifidobacteria colonize the large intestine. Some of the bad bacteria include *E.coli, Streptococci*, and *Helicobacter pylori.*[12] The less healthy bacteria can produce enzymes or proteases that break down the brush borders of the intestines, leading to damage of the intestinal wall. The good bacteria crowd the spaces along the intestinal walls to decrease the likelihood of the less beneficial bacteria adhering to and damaging the walls.

Leaky gut syndrome describes the formation of small openings in the intestinal wall that allow undigested food particles to pass through the openings and into the bloodstream. One of the most common culprits for this condition is *Helicobacter pylori*. These bacteria cause stomach ulcers and bore into tissues. Once in the bloodstream, the food particles act as foreign invaders or toxins to the immune system, which in turn is activated to gobble them up. This cascade of events is the reason behind food allergies and other symptoms associated with food sensitivities. When the immune system is always "turned on," it becomes exhausting for the individual, and can lead to symptoms such as chronic fatigue, frequent colds, flu and autoimmune disease.

The following is a list of symptoms and conditions commonly associated with dysbiosis and leaky gut syndrome:

- Headaches
- Irritable bowel syndrome, gas and bloating, Crohn's, colitis
- Chronic fatigue
- Fibromyalgia
- Eczema, psoriasis, rosacea, cradle cap, diaper rash, vitiligo
- Chronic urinary tract infections, herpes, yeast infections, endometriosis, cervical dysplasia, prostatitis, benign prostatic hypertrophy
- Allergies, asthma
- Chronic sinusitis, ear infections
- Arthritis

- Autoimmune disease
- Cancer

The Immune System Link to GI Tract

Half of our immune system is in our gut. The gut-associated lymphoid tissue (GALT) is present in the intestines. GALT is lymphoid tissue that is comprised of:

- Peyer's Patches (specialized immune cells in the intestines)
- Lymph tissue that accumulates with age in the stomach and intestines[13]

If the GI tract is loaded with unhealthy bacteria, the immune system may be compromised, which allows more pathogenic bacteria to survive. This vicious cycle repeats and is often evident in people who have the dual symptoms of digestive complaints and lowered immunity. When you repair and re-inoculate the gut with probiotics (good gut bacteria), the immune system improves.

Allergies are another common manifestation of impaired GI tract function and leaky gut syndrome. If you heal what is happening in the gut, generally, the allergies disappear. In an allergic patient, the immune system is always on stand-by. It is hypersensitive, and ready to launch an attack at the slightest threat of a foreign particle, including dust, pollens, moulds, pet dander, and so on. When the dysbiosis in the gut is treated effectively with probiotics, anti-fungal/bacterial remedies and dietary changes, the hyperactivity of the immune system is toned down, and the patient no longer reacts to the allergens.

How to Detoxify the GI Tract

One of the best ways to stimulate the immunity and Peyer's patches in the GI tract is by using a castor oil pack on the abdomen, three times a week. To make a castor oil pack, buy a bottle of organic, cold-pressed castor oil and a cotton or wool, unbleached cloth. Soak about one half cup castor oil on the cloth and scrunch the cloth to try to evenly distribute the oil. Then place the cloth on the abdomen and cover with plastic wrap. Place a hot water bottle on top of the plastic and let it sit for forty-five minutes to an hour. You can then keep the cloth in a glass jar and reuse next time, adding more castor oil if necessary.
(See Chapter One: Detoxification of the Body; How to Detoxify the GI Tract).

CASE study

Marvin, a twenty-two-year-old male, had had allergies all his life. He used inhalers for asthma, which would come and go with the allergens of the season. He was lethargic and lacked motivation or a zest for life. I finally convinced him to go on a gluten-free and dairy-free diet, which has a low allergenic reactivity. This type of diet is very restrictive and is not for everyone, especially those who are used to eating out a lot or who do not have the time to prepare meals for themselves. He took some probiotics and Citricidal (an extract of grapefruit seeds) to kill any fungus and bad gut bacteria. Marvin started to notice that his allergies were slowly getting better and he wasn't as reactive as he used to be. After a month of being completely gluten and dairy-free, his allergies disappeared.

Sceptics may say that he outgrew his allergies. I thought the same thing myself until Marvin reported that the few times he cheated on his diet, his allergies started to come back again, including his asthma.

Fibre

Fibre is important for cleaning out the intestines and increasing the size of the stool. Fibre helps to regulate the transit time of the stool. You can determine your transit time by eating something that will show up visibly in the stool, such as kernels of corn or beets. Take note of the time between eating the food and when it appears in the stool. A normal transit time is approximately twenty-four hours. If it takes longer than this, your stool is not moving through the large intestine fast enough.

People think that if they have one bowel movement (BM) a day, they are normal. However, I urge women to have at least two BMs a day, and men three a day (since usually men eat more than women). If you have a slow transit time, you may only be moving stool out of the last part of the intestine with every bowel movement and the rest is left sitting. The longer feces sits in the colon, the more toxic it becomes.

I usually recommend increasing one's fibre to at least thirty-five grams a day. There are two types of fibre, both insoluble and soluble. The following chart gives examples of each type of fibre.

SOLUBLE	INSOLUBLE
(Pectins, gums, mucilages, hemi-celluloses) Helps fermentation in GI tract Increases cholesterol absorption and excretion	(Cellulose and hemi-cellulose) Increase bulk of stools and decrease toxicity in colon
Apples Bananas Oranges Potatoes Cabbage Carrots Grapes Oatmeal Oatbran Sesame seeds Flaxseeds Psyllium	Wheat bran Apple/pears with peel Strawberries Raw carrots Whole grain breads

Coffee enema

A direct way of cleansing the last part of the GI tract is with a coffee enema. This is a technique I only prescribe in extreme cases of constipation. Coffee stimulates the contractions of the colon walls, thus expelling any fecal matter that is retained. It also stimulates the liver and gallbladder to secrete more bile and increase detoxification.

To prepare and perform a coffee enema:

To prepare and perform a coffee enema:

1. Add three tablespoons of ground organic coffee beans to four cups of distilled water in a stainless steel or glass pot.
2. Boil the coffee for three minutes then let simmer for twenty minutes. Strain coffee and allow liquid to cool to body temperature or when it feels slightly hotter than comfortable to the touch.
3. Fill a rectal bulb syringe with the strained liquid coffee solution. (Note: you will have plenty left over that you can store in the

fridge in a covered glass jar and reheat it on the stove for next use).

4. Lie in a warm bathtub on your side. Relax. Then gently insert the end of the rectal bulb into the anus. Slowly squeeze the coffee into the rectum and retain it as long as possible.
5. Move to the toilet and have a bowel movement as soon as you cannot retain the enema any longer.
6. Repeat the enema as prescribed by your naturopathic doctor – as different conditions and levels of toxicity require either more or less frequent enemas.
7. The rectal bulb can be disinfected in water mixed with Citricidal (grapefruit seed extract) or tea tree oil. Mix five drops of either in two cups hot water and let sit five minutes.
8. Some minerals are lost during an enema, so it is important to replenish lost minerals with plenty of fresh fruits and vegetables, or a mineral supplement.

Contraindications for the coffee enema include pregnancy, young children, gallstones, hemorrhoids, acute inflammatory bowel disease, or history of sexual abuse. Always check with your naturopathic doctor before attempting a coffee enema.

Herbal medicine for the GI tract

Herbs for the GI tract are usually laxatives. Some anti-microbial herbs are also useful for clearing bacteria, parasites and fungi from the gut. Psyllium husks are unique in that they act like little brushes that sweep the inner lining of the gut mucosa, and increase the bulk of the stool. The chart on the next page lists some of these herbs and their uses.

HERBAL MEDICINE	PART USED	PROPERTIES	ADULT DOSAGE	CONTRAINDICATIONS
Cascara sagrada (Rhamnus purshiana)	Dried bark	Gentle laxative, bitter tonic	15 - 30 drops of tincture at bedtime	Pregnancy and lactation
Senna (Senna alexandrina)	Dried fruit pods	Strong laxative	15 - 20 drops of tincture 3 times daily between meals	Pregnancy and lactation
Peppermint (Mentha piperita)	Leaves and flowers	Antiseptic, antispasmodic, carminative, analgesic	Tea: pour a cup of boiling water over a heaping teaspoon of dried herb and infuse for 10 minutes, covered, drink 3 times a day between meals	Pregnancy and lactation
Marshmallow (Althaea officinalis)	Root	Demulcent, soothes irritation in the GI tract, helpful for any irritation, inflammation, e.g., IBS, colitis, Crohn's	20 - 30 drops tincture, 3 times a day between meals	
Oregano	Oil from the leaves	Antiseptic, antiparasitic, antifungal	Emulsified tablets are absorbed best (e.g., Biotics A.D.P.), 1 tablet 3 times a day just after a meal	Pregnancy and lactation, stomach ulcers, intestinal bleeding, liver disease
Psyllium	Husks	Fibre source, cleanses inner lining of intestinal tract	Start with ¼ tsp at bedtime with 8 oz. water, slowly work up to 2 tsp	Do not take with other supplements or medications because their absorption will be affected

Function of the Kidneys

The kidneys are thought of by most as the organs that produce urine, whereas, their main function is blood filtration and detoxification. The kidneys receive twenty-five per cent of the body's total blood volume. They redistribute ninety-nine per cent of the volume of blood back into circulation. The kidneys are responsible for filtering the by-products of protein metabolism and only 0.1 per cent of the filtered blood becomes urine. The kidneys excrete toxins from the liver that have been bio-transformed by Phase 2 enzymes.

It is very common for successful and busy people to neglect drinking enough pure water and urinating as needed. If these basic needs are not met, the kidneys develop toxicity over time and their filtration ability is decreased.

Kidney detoxification starts with drinking plenty of pure water and urinating frequently. The body can only absorb between two and four ounces of water at a time. Anything more is excreted in the urine immediately. This is why I tell my patients to sip small amounts of water throughout the day and not all at once. You should not wait until you are thirsty to drink. By that time, you are already dehydrated. This is the formula for water consumption:

One ounce of water per kilogram of bodyweight per day.

So for example, a woman weighing fifty-five kilograms would need to drink fifty-five ounces of water a day. A glass being eight ounces, this works out to approximately seven glasses a day. The same is true for infants and the elderly. More water should be consumed during breastfeeding, pregnancy and if you exercise.

Symptoms of kidney toxicity are as follows:

- Infrequent urination
- Frequent urination
- Dark circles or puffiness under the eyes
- Edema or swelling
- Kidney pain
- Kidney stones*

* Kidney stones are toxic accumulations that get stuck and conjoin in the kidney.

One cannot form kidney stones without having previous toxicity in the kidney. The colour of your urine should be light yellow. If it is dark yellow, you are dehydrated. If it is clear, you are drinking too much at once. Keep in mind that some B vitamins will make the urine a fluorescent yellow.

Kidney Detoxification With Food

Beets help to cleanse the kidneys.
Parsley is a kidney detoxifier.
Dandelion leaves are diuretic, meaning they increase the flow of urine, but do not deplete potassium from the body as many pharmaceutical diuretics do.
Watermelon is a natural diuretic. The seeds can be ground and used as a kidney cleanser.
Cucumbers are naturally diuretic.
Barley is a grain that acts to rid the body of excess water retention.

Herbal Remedies for Kidney Detoxification[14]

HERBAL MEDICINE	PART USED	PROPERTIES	ADULT DOSE	CONTRAINDICATIONS
Dandelion (Taraxacum officinale)	Leaf	Diuretic that does not deplete potassium	20 - 30 drops tincture, 3 times a day, eat raw leaves in salad	
Horsetail (Equisetum arvense)	Dried stems	Diuretic, astringent, high in silica, good for hair and nails	20 - 30 drops of tincture 3 times a day, between meals	Pregnancy
Bearberry (Arctostaphylos uva-ursi)	Leaves	Diuretic, astringent, antilithic, dissolves kidney stones		
Yarrow (Achillea millefolium)	Leaves and flowers	Diuretic, antiseptic, hypotensive		Low blood pressure
Stone Root (Collinsonia canadensis)	Root and rhizome	Antilithic, diuretic, diaphoretic	20 - 30 drops 3 times a day, between meals	
Gravel Root (Eupatorium purpureum)	Root and rhizome	Antilithic, diuretic	15 - 20 drops of tincture, 3 times a day between meals	

***Many of the herbs mentioned above are found in my formulation VitaDetox™ from VitaTree™ Nutritionals. See www.vitatree.ca for more information**

Definitions of herbal properties:
Antilithic: Dissolves stones and prevents stone formation
Antiseptic: Destroys unwanted micro-organisms
Astringent: Contracts tissues and decreases secretions and discharges
Diaphoretic: Promotes perspiration
Diuretic: Aids in increasing the flow of urine

Note: Water retention in the body can be due to sluggish kidneys, but may also be due to heart failure or hormonal imbalances. It is important to find the root cause of water retention before treatment with diuretics.

Function of the Lymphatic System

The function of the lymphatic system is to remove waste and fluid from the tissues (interstitial fluid) to the blood. The lymphatic system also plays a big role in the functioning of the immune system.

Lymph has collection points called lymph nodes. This is where the cells of the immune system do their work to clean up cellular debris, bacteria and toxins.

Lymphatic fluid flows most effectively when the body is active and breathing. The lymph system does not have its own circulatory system as the blood does, so it requires the contractions of muscles in the body for it to flow properly. Lymph movement is also helped by changes in intra-thoracic pressure caused by breathing. If the lymph is not stimulated to contract, it can become backed up, thus, slowing the detoxification process.

How to Detoxify the Lymph

Lymph congestion is more common in those who are sedentary and do not exercise. One of the best exercises to improve lymphatic flow is rebounding on a mini-trampoline. Deep breathing exercises help to move the lymph. This is one reason why exercises such as yoga and Pilates are so great at detoxification. Not only are you moving the lymph by the movement of the skeletal muscles, but the combined effect of the deep breathing makes the lymph flow even more efficiently. Lymph flow can also be improved by lymphatic massage by a qualified practitioner.

Herbal Medicine for the Lymphatic System
Cleavers
(Galium aparine)
Part used: Dried aerial parts
Properties: Lymphatic tonic, diuretic, anti-inflammatory
Standard adult dose: Tincture, fifteen to thirty drops, three times a day, between meals.
Tea: Pour one cup of boiling water over three teaspoons dried herb and let stand for ten minutes. Drink two to three times a day.[15]

Homeopathic remedies for the Lymphatic system
Phytolacca
Take a 30C or K potency, one pellet, twice daily under the tongue for three days. Stop sooner, if symptoms disappear.

Cell Detoxification
Every cell has the capacity and tools to detoxify. Cells take in toxins and then either transform, neutralize, or excrete them to the substance outside the cells, known as the matrix, or extracellular space. The matrix allows for the passage of things into the cell. If the matrix is healthy, the cell is healthy. The matrix detoxifies substances and prevents them from entering the cell. If the matrix becomes overloaded with toxins or too acidic, it can no longer protect the cell and the toxins are free to enter.

The matrix also sets the stage for cellular growth. Cellular growth needs to be in the correct order. If it is not, it can be called cancer. A clean matrix will allow orderly growth, whereas a toxic matrix will promote disordered growth because the messages it receives become scrambled. The matrix drains into the lymph system, which drains via the kidneys.

Each cell of the body contains Phase 1 and Phase 2 enzyme systems for detoxification. Phase 1 enzymes generally transform a toxin into something that can be further detoxified by Phase 2 enzymes. These toxins that are bio-transformed may end up being slightly more toxic than their original state. For this reason, it is very important that the Phase 2 enzymes are working well and nutritionally supported to carry out their functions. Nutrients to support Phase 1 and Phase 2 enzymes are as follows:

PHASE 1 DETOXIFICATION MODULATORS	PHASE 2 DETOXIFICATION MODULATORS
Vitamin B1 Vitamin B2 Vitamin B3 Vitamin C Folic acid Flavonoids (cruciferous vegetables) Phospholipids Indole 3 carbinol (cabbage, broccoli, cauliflower) Coumarins Methylxanthines (coffee, chocolate)	Flavonoids (cruciferous vegetables) Indole 3 carbinol (cabbage, broccoli, cauliflower) Carnosic acid (rosemary) Diallyl sulfides (garlic) Isoflavones (soy) Ellagic acid (red grape skin) Curcumin (turmeric) Monoterpenoids (citrus)

CHAPTER 2 | DIET

After interviewing many millionaires, I have come to the conclusion that they either eat very well, or they do not eat well at all. Very few seem to lie in the middle. As people become more successful, they may have more money to spend on organic, higher quality foods. Others spend more money eating out, which may be responsible for hidden toxins, fats and sugar. Those on the other end of the spectrum may eat very little due to hectic schedules, which leads to bypassing meals and consuming coffee and cookies instead.

There are many toxic exposures we can't control in our lives, such as the air we breathe, toxins we were exposed to in utero, and through our mother's milk if we were breastfed. However, there are some toxins we can choose to avoid and have some control over their influence in our lives. The foods we choose in our diets are one of the potential toxin sources that we have some control over. Unfortunately, even organic foods have become toxic. They are affected by nearby runoffs of industry wastes and toxicity. However, I still believe that organic is better than pesticide-laden, non-organic foods.

The key to a healthy diet is everything in moderation. I give numerous lectures to businessmen and businesswomen about detoxification and healthy eating. Many of the attendees are shocked to find out that much of what they are eating is not healthy. However, the key is to still enjoy food, but to make healthier choices when buying and preparing it. There are plenty of healthy substitutes for foods that we are accustomed to eating. It does take some effort at first to become familiar with food products that we may not know a lot about. But with a bit of practise, grocery shopping and cooking soon becomes a routine, and little effort is needed to find the healthier choices.

What is the Best Diet?
Unfortunately, there is no single diet that is right for everyone. Trends in the nutrition industry generally lead the masses to whatever is the "in" diet of the year. The low-fat diet in the 1980s was over-prescribed, and we can now see the consequences. Today, the high-protein diet with low carbohydrates is the new trend. However, this too can be detrimental to some people. I always stress that diets are very individual. Our diets should match our biochemical individuality. So how do you find out what is best for you? Intuition is always your best guide. However, if

your intuition is not yet accurate enough, I would recommend the advice of a practitioner who can test food sensitivities and prescribe a diet that fits your tastes and lifestyle.

General Guidelines for Healthy Eating

Even though there is no one diet that would suit everyone, there are some general guidelines for healthy eating. You would be best to avoid what I call the "white foods," which include white flour, sugar and salt. Any refined carbohydrate has been so altered by processing that its original nutritional value has been lost, and can be harmful for the body.

Processed grains, in particular, lose their enzymes, vitamins and minerals, which are essential for their proper digestion and absorption. A diet filled with these foods can lead to toxicity in the digestive tract and improper elimination. Plus, the essential vitamins and nutrients that supply all other body processes are limited, resulting in overall malnutrition.

Refined Sugar

The refining of sugar produces sucrose, which is not a natural element for the body to metabolize. Refined sugar is robbed of its essential nutrients – fibre, protein, water, vitamins and minerals. These nutrients help in the metabolism of the sugar in its raw form. When they are removed, the body needs to supply these nutrients from other places to try to break down the sucrose. Sugar also depletes your immune system. The pancreas secretes insulin in response to sugar in the blood. Increased insulin production causes a decrease in growth hormone secretion from the pituitary, and growth hormone is essential for immune function. Too much sugar also causes the body to become too acidic, which causes the calcium and magnesium (which are basic, the opposite to acidic) stored in the bones and other tissues to enter the bloodstream from the bones – thus, potentially, leading to osteoporosis.

Sugar was once a very pure, natural sweetener. Nowadays, sugar has been so adulterated that on its own it can cause disease. Processed sugar causes bacteria to multiply in the body, and even feeds cancer cells.

Coffee and Caffeine Products

Coffee is the one of the most widely consumed beverages in the world. Unfortunately, it has many negative side effects, which most people are not aware of. Coffee is comprised of over 100 different chemicals – some naturally occurring, some synthetic, from pesticides and chemical sprays. Nitrosomines are chemicals naturally found in coffee beans that are the same co-carcinogens used in the curing of meats and bacon. One of the main culprits for health problems is caffeine. One cup of coffee contains between fifty and 180 mg of caffeine. The chart on the next page summarizes the amounts of caffeine in common sources:

SOURCE OF CAFFEINE	Mg OF CAFFEINE PER SERVING
Coffee (6 oz. serving)	
Automatic drip	180
Automatic perk	125
Instant	75
Decaffeinated	5
Coffee-flavoured instant mixes	50
Cocoa (6 oz. serving)	11
Tea (6 oz. serving)	
Black	75
Green	32
Decaffeinated	1
Soft drinks (12 oz. servings) Coke, Pepsi	45

Caffeine is a stimulant that belongs to a class of chemicals called methyl xanthines. These chemicals act on the nervous and endocrine systems. In the nervous system, methyl xanthines decrease the threshold for nerve firing, thus increasing the nerve conduction.

They also block receptors for adenosine, a molecule that decreases alertness, heart activity and respiration rate. By blocking adenosine, alertness is enhanced, as well as heart and respiration rates. This is one of the reasons caffeine is used by athletes before a competition (whether legally or not) to increase their performance.[16]

Caffeine has many other effects on the body:

- Irritation to the GI tract and liver, because it stimulates the secretion of stomach acid, which increases the risk of peptic ulcers
- Diuretic, causing a loss of water, potassium, magnesium, zinc, B vitamins and vitamin C in the urine
- May cause diarrhea, as it is a relaxant to the smooth muscle in the colon
- Decreases the absorption of iron and calcium, possibly leading to osteoporosis
- Affects the heart by temporarily increasing blood pressure, increases cholesterol, may cause arrhythmias
- In pregnancy, causes fetal heart rate to rise
- Linked to fibrocystic breast disease
- Narcotic, belonging to the same chemical alkaloid group as morphine, nicotine, cocaine and strychnine
- Stimulant, which requires increasing dosage to obtain the same effects after chronic use

However, coffee does have some benefits as well:

- Increases bowel movements, linked to a decrease in colon cancer
- Temporary increase in brain function and energy levels
- Increases fat loss by lipolysis, or the breakdown of fats
- Bitter taste stimulates liver function
- Increases Phase 1 liver detoxification
- Antioxidants

If you do drink coffee, the best type to consume is shade-grown, organic, bird-preserving coffee. This type of coffee is in its most natural form, shaded by larger trees that overhang the coffee beans. In this natural state, the forest ecosystem and inhabitant birds are preserved, whereas in other operations, sun-grown plants are cultivated and do not support the environmental milieu for other species to live.[17]

Decaffeinated coffee may even be worse than regular coffee because most processes of decaffeination include the use of solvents, notably trichloroethylene, a close relative of the plastic chemical vinyl chloride, which can cause a rare type of liver cancer. Trichloroethylene is a solvent used in dry cleaning and an industrial degreaser for metals. It is also found in paint removers and carpet cleaners. You can buy coffee that is naturally decaffeinated by a water or Swiss water process, in which no chemicals are used.

Coffee beans can be mouldy and aggravate people with chronic fungal infections or candidiasis. The roasting of coffee beans decreases mould, but may still be a factor. Decaffeinated coffee may have more mould than regular coffee, as caffeine acts as a natural antifungal.

In terms of detoxification, coffee increases the cytochrome p450 Phase 1 detoxification. This can be good if your Phase 2 is in good working order. However, if your Phase 2 is slow or underactive, you are likely to create more toxic metabolites from Phase 1.

Beware if you want to stop drinking coffee "cold turkey." You will likely develop headaches if you do not cut down your consumption of caffeinated beverages gradually. I usually recommend that people cut down by a half a cup a week. For instance, if you usually consume three cups of coffee a day, for the first week, decrease it to two and a half cups. The next week, have only two cups, and so on, until you are off it completely.

However, some people are not willing to give up coffee entirely. They feel it is one of their only "treats" left after changing their diet and eating more healthfully. In such a case, I think it is okay to have two or three coffees – organic shade-grown – a week, if possible. If it is decaf, it should be naturally decaffeinated or Swiss water process.

Wheat

The wheat grain has been altered so much over the past fifty years that it has become very difficult to digest. Wheat gluten – which is a protein particle of the grain – causes digestive distress for many people, not just those with celiac disease. Most people find that if they cut wheat out of their diet for even a few weeks, they notice an increase in energy, a decrease in bloating and gas, and usually improvements in the other symptoms, which were their chief complaint. Unfortunately, wheat is one of the most difficult foods to eliminate from a North American diet because it is everywhere, and in everything. With this in mind, I sometimes suggest that a patient eliminates wheat from the diet for six of the seven days in a week, and on their "cheat day" they can have as much as they want to. Keeping in mind that the next day after a wheat binge, they will probably feel lethargic and bloated.

There are many alternative grains to wheat:

- Amaranth
- Quinoa
- Spelt
- Rye
- Rice
- Millet
- Oat
- Corn
- Kamut
- Arrowroot
- Buckwheat

In general, these grains can be used as substitutes for wheat, either as a flour or the whole grain. It is important to note that those with gluten sensitivity must avoid some of these grains, as they still contain gluten. Some gluten-free alternatives are:

- Rice
- Corn
- Arrowroot
- Buckwheat
- Potato
- Tapioca

Gluten-free flours tend to be heavier and drier than glutinous flours, because it's the gluten that gives the flour part of its leavening and stickiness. When using gluten-free flour in baking, you may need to experiment with a combination of flours to get the consistency you are looking for.

It may be a good idea to purchase a bread-maker and bake your own bread at home. Homemade bread is healthier than store-bought bread because it doesn't have any preservatives, and you control the wholeness of the ingredients included. I make my own spelt bread at home and other organic breads in ten minutes of preparation time.

Nothing tastes or smells better than home-baked bread.

Milk and Dairy Products

Dairy products today are not what they used to be. The care of cattle has changed over the years, and cows are now inundated with medications and hormones to maximize milk production. Humans are the only species of mammal that drink the milk of another species. Cow milk is meant for their calves. Calves double their weight in forty-seven days, whereas human babies double in 180 days. Calves also weigh approximately 300 pounds after one year. Clearly, the milk from cows differs in composition to human milk to supply the needs of such rapid growth in calves. Human milk is meant for humans, and only in the first few years of life.

Dairy products have been marketed to make the consumer believe they are our best protection against osteoporosis. This misinformation has probably led to higher rates of osteoporosis in dairy-consuming populations. If you look at some African tribeswomen, their dairy consumption is next to zero and they breastfeed over five children, usually for more than two years each, with no osteoporosis. You have to ask yourself if dairy is what it is cracked up to be.

One of the reasons that dairy products may even contribute to osteoporosis is that they are high in animal protein. Animal protein is acid forming in the blood. This acid in the blood needs to be buffered, in order to maintain the proper pH. So what buffers the blood? Calcium. This calcium often comes out of the bones to do this job. Canadians and Americans consume the highest amount of dairy products, as well as the United Kingdom and Scandinavia. It is ironic that these are also the countries with the highest osteoporosis rates.

The type of calcium in dairy products may also be a factor. The body only utilizes organic calcium from fruits, grains and vegetables. The type of calcium in dairy products is inorganic calcium. Inorganic calcium is removed from the blood and collected in the kidneys (causing kidney stones) and not used for building bone matrix.

List of non-dairy sources of calcium[18]

FOOD	AMOUNT	MG OF CALCIUM
Turnip greens, cooked	1 cup	492
Lamb's quarters, cooked	1 cup	490
Sardines, with bones	3 oz.	372
Collard greens, cooked	1 cup	357
Rhubarb, cooked	1 cup	348
Spinach, cooked	1 cup	276
Oatmeal, fortified	1 cup	208
Salmon	3.5 oz.	185
Tofu, firm	2/3 cup	190
Broccoli, cooked	1 cup	180
Fortified soy milk	1 cup	167
Dandelion greens	1/2 cup	147
Molasses, black strap	1 tablespoon	137
Almonds	1/4 cup	92
Orange	1 medium	52
Spinach, raw	1 cup	44
Tahini	2 tablespoons	42

The quality of the milk is only as healthy as the cow it came from. It is common for dairy farm cattle to get breast infections or mastitis because of the constant tugging at their teats from milking machines. These cows then need repeated rounds of antibiotics to clear the infections. These antibiotics are in the milk and may lead to antibiotic-resistant strains of bacteria in humans.

In my practice, these are the most common clinical problems that are the result of over-consumption of dairy products:

- Chronic childhood ear infections
- Eczema
- Colic in infants
- Upper respiratory infections
- Headaches

- Sinusitis
- Constipation
- Osteoporosis

Dairy products are mucous-forming and often the culprit in chronic sinusitis and colds. If someone is sensitive to dairy, they usually have a threshold amount that they can tolerate; anything above this amount causes their symptoms to return. Some people confuse the term milk intolerance or sensitivity to lactose intolerance.

Lactose is a milk sugar that becomes difficult to digest as we grow older. We have the highest amount of lactase (the enzyme to break down and digest lactose) when we are babies, and it decreases as we age. Can you guess why? We are only meant to drink milk from our mothers in the first few years of life. After that, our need for lactase decreases naturally. But you can have a milk sensitivity that has nothing to do with lactose. Some people are sensitive to either the whey or the casein in dairy products, and not the lactose. Therefore, those who have been diagnosed with a dairy sensitivity should avoid all forms of dairy, including "hidden" forms of dairy in the following ingredients:

- Casein
- Caseinate
- Sodium caseinate
- Calcium caseinate
- Lactose
- Whey
- Lactalbumin
- Cream
- Milk solids

Animal Products

Animal products are becoming more and more toxic. The animals raised for human consumption are only as healthy as what they eat. Farmers today are feeding these animals more and more chemicals and grains that are not part of their normal diet. For instance, cows eat primarily grass, but farmers allow them to eat grains and meats to increase their size and fat content. Animal products are also high in saturated fats, which we all know are not the best choice for our health. Organic or free-range meat is always a better choice, and a good investment for your physical health. Non-organic meats are full of antibiotics, which are given to the animals for infection and hormones to increase the size and fat content of the animal. The more fat, the more tender and juicy the meat. Unfortunately, the hormones are stored in the animal fats, and this is one reason to stay away from them.

Meats also contribute to an unbalanced and unhealthy gut environment. Putrefaction occurs in the intestines of people who consume a lot of meat and animal fat. This type of diet increases the bacteroides species of gut bacteria, which is not beneficial and leads to dysbiosis. Studies show that this type of diet is implicated in the formation of colon and breast cancer.

Dark Green, Leafy Vegetables

I can't say enough positive things about dark green, leafy vegetables. They should be the staple of everyone's diet. They help to cleanse the liver and blood; they stimulate digestive enzyme secretion; they provide important phytonutrients and chlorophyll, and they are low in calories and high in fibre. Chlorophyll is a molecule that has the ability to bind heavy metals in the body.

Green, leafy vegetables contain essential fatty acids, namely omega-3 fats that are important for proper cell detoxification and brain function, and are anti-inflammatory. If that isn't enough, they improve your skin, keep you thin, and give you lots of energy. So, what's not to love? I usually recommend six cups of raw (works out to about three cups steamed) dark, leafy greens a day. My favourites include rapini, bok choy, Swiss chard, dandelion greens, romaine, kale and spinach. These should all be organic, whenever possible.

Brassica Family of Vegetables

The brassica family of vegetables include cabbage, Brussel sprouts, cauliflower, broccoli, kale, bok choy, rapini, kohlrabi, rutabagas, garden sorrel, watercress, collards, radish, mustard and turnips. They contain a plant chemical known as indole-3-carbinol (I3C) that inhibits Phase 1 detoxification in the liver and increases Phase 2 detoxification. I3Cs are particularly important in hormonal imbalance disorders, especially when there is too much estrogen in relation to progesterone in the body, also known as estrogen dominance. I3Cs are helpful in the conversion of estrogen to a less toxic metabolite. Estrogen is converted in the liver to either a C2 estrogen metabolite, a C4, or a C16 estrogen metabolite. The C2 is more healthy and readily excreted by the body, whereas C4 and C16 estrogens are toxic. C16 estrogens are active estrogens and can induce breast cancers in animals. The brassica foods help to form more of the C2 estrogen, which is protective against breast cancer.[19]

One half cup to one cup of the brassica family foods can be eaten daily. They should be eaten raw or lightly steamed. People with hypothyroidism need to steam the brassicas, because they can interfere with thyroid function.

Essential Fatty Acids

Some fats are termed essential fatty acids (EFAs) because our bodies do not produce them. They are healthy fats that are required by the body for a number of important functions. The three main groups of EFAs are omega-3, omega-6 and omega-9.

ESSENTIAL FATTY ACIDS	BEST SOURCES	FUNCTIONS
Omega-3 Alpha-linolenic acid (LNA)	flaxseeds, black currant seeds, cold water fish, hemp seeds, pumpkin seeds, soy, dark green leafy vegetables	Eicosopentanoic acid (EPA) and decosahexanoic acid (DHA) are omega-3 fats found in cold water fish such as salmon, trout, mackerel, sardines EPA and DHA help keep cell walls healthy and improve brain function and development
Omega-6 Linoleic Acid	safflower, sunflower, borage, soy, walnut, sesame seed, black currant seed, evening primrose oil, corn and wheat	GLA is an omega-6 oil found in evening primrose oil, black currant oil, borage oil and mother's milk GLA has the benefit of bypassing a potential block in the formation of healthy prostaglandins that can arise when linolenic and linoleic fatty acids are metabolized
Omega-9 Oleic Acid	olive oil, almond, pecan, cashew, hazelnut, macadamia nuts	Helps to maintain cell wall structure and function

Functions of EFAs

EFAs maintain the proper cell wall structure. Cell walls are made of phospholipids, which need healthy fats to remain pliable. When cell walls are pliable, they allow metabolic processes and detoxification to occur more efficiently. If the cell walls become rigid (from trans-fatty acids and superheated fats), detoxification slows in affected cells.

EFAs are essential for proper brain development and hormone

synthesis. They fulfil these functions:

- Protect cell walls from carcinogenic materials
- Essential for brain and nerve development
- Help in oxygen transfer and energy production
- Precursors for hormone synthesis
- Precursors for fifty chemical messengers, called prostaglandins
- Prostaglandins are hormone-like chemicals that affect the function of many cells in the body. They are made from unsaturated fatty acids. In nutrition, the three most commonly discussed prostaglandins are series one, two and three. Series one and three prostaglandins (PG1) and (PG3) are anti-inflammatory (good guys), whereas, series two prostaglandins (PG2) are pro-inflammatory (bad guys).

The various prostaglandins have the following functions:

- Made by every cell
- Influence platelet aggregation
- Regulate inflammation
- Influence cholesterol synthesis
- Influence triglycerides
- Inhibit tumour growth
- Influences cell membrane permeability
- Smooth muscle relaxation and contraction
- Blood pressure changes[20]

Symptoms of EFA deficiency include the following:

- Vision loss
- Learning disabilities
- Tingling in arms and legs
- Joint pain
- Loss of motor coordination
- Slowed growth
- Dry skin
- Dermatitis
- Hormonal irregularities
- Hair loss

Fish

Fish are a good source of digestible protein and essential fats. The further along the food chain, the more easily digestible the food. For instance, pork meat is the closest to human flesh and, therefore, the most difficult to digest. Fish, however, are furthest along the food chain and the most easily digested non-vegetarian protein.

The main concern these days is heavy metal toxicity in fish. The longer a fish lives, where it swims and the more fat it accumulates, all have a bearing on its potential toxicity. Generally, cold-water ocean fish are the best. I tend to discourage patients from buying farmed fish. These fish are usually genetically altered and are known to be high in disease, due to overcrowding in the farmed water. Farmed fish are also high in polychlorinated biphenyls (PCBs) that are given in their feed. (PCBs are defined as any of a family of industrial compounds produced by chlorination of biphenyls. They are known environmental pollutants that accumulate in animal tissues. PCBs are highly toxic, and are linked to diseases such as cancer and reproductive abnormalities).

All food has energy, whether it is derived from plants or animals. We absorb the energy from foods, as well as the physical nutrients. From an energetic standpoint, I think a fish from the ocean where it swims freely has more positive energy than a fish that is bred to be consumed by humans in an overcrowded pond or tank.

From a nutritional perspective, many fish contain eicosapentaenoic acid (EPA) and docosahexaenoic acid (DHA), which are essential fatty acids important for lowering cholesterol, and protecting from hardening of the arteries, or atherosclerosis. Both EPA and DHA can be formed by the body, but certain conditions and nutritional deficiencies slow down the conversion of omega-3 fatty acids into them. For this reason, it is beneficial to get pre-formed EPA and DHA from fish oils.[21]

These fish have the highest percentages of EPA and DHA:
- Salmon
- Sardines
- Mackerel
- Trout
- Eel

Unfortunately, some of these fish have high levels of mercury, so should be eaten in moderation (See Chapter Five: Heavy Metal Toxicity; Sources of Mercury).

The dosage for essential fatty acids usually varies according to a patient's needs. One major advantage of supplementing fish oils over

vegetarian sources of essential fatty acids is they are already converted to EPA and DHA. Some people have difficulty converting omega-3 fats to these compounds.
Fish oils can be taken in capsule form – one capsule, three times a day, with food.

Fish oil supplements can be potentially hazardous. The essential fats are very sensitive to heat, air and light. If there is any hint of a fishy taste or smell, the fish oil may be rancid and should be thrown. I recommend that patients open one of their fish oil capsules to test for taste and smell. If it is at all fishy, it should not be consumed. The manufacturing of fish oil supplements should be in a cold temperature environment, in the dark and guaranteed to be free of heavy metals.

Organic Food
Organic foods are always preferable to pesticide-laden and genetically altered foods. Certified organic means that the food is grown without pesticides or herbicides, and passes inspection according to the laws of organic farming. Organic farmers use crop rotation, mulching and manure to keep their crops healthy. They also use predator insects to keep unwanted pests off their crops. This all leads to healthier soils, less soil erosion and a higher quality crop. The "organic" label also ensures that the products have not been irradiated.

The problem with synthetic pesticides and herbicides is that they are toxic chemicals. These toxins enter our systems and need to be eliminated. The way that I see it is this: we are exposed to uncontrollable toxins every day in our environment and through the air we breathe. Food is one area in which we have some degree of choice, in terms of our exposure to toxins. Eating organic foods is a positive investment in our health, and prevention of disease. If organic options aren't available, make sure to wash some of the pesticides off non-organic produce with something like Natural Fruit and Veggie Wash by Nature Clean.

Digestive Enzymes
Digestive enzymes are either secreted by our bodies, or can be supplied in supplement form. Their purpose is to help break down and digest our food. As we age, our own digestive enzymes decrease in strength. If we are under stress, our nervous system will not allow the normal secretion of these enzymes. I will usually prescribe enzymes for short periods of time to help someone jump-start his or her digestive system.

The three categories of digestive enzymes in the body are amylases (to break down starches and sugars), proteases (to break down proteins) and lipases (to break down fats). Enzymes occur naturally in foods, but are rendered inactive if heated. This is why it is important to consume raw foods as much as possible, to help with digestion. Foods that are naturally high in enzymes include avocado, papaya, pineapple, mango, banana and sprouts.

Digestive enzymes can be taken in supplement form to aid digestion. Some of these products are derived from animal sources, such as pancreatin and pepsin. Other enzymes are obtained from aspergillus, a fungus. I usually discourage patients with a yeast or candida problem from using the fungus-derived enzymes.

Digestive enzymes are helpful for those whose digestive system is sluggish. I don't recommend long-term use of enzyme supplements because the body gets accustomed to the supplement and may decrease its own secretion of enzymes over time. A good-quality enzyme will include amylases, proteases, lipases and hydrochloric acid (HCL). HCL is stomach acid that aids in the digestion of proteins. (HCL is not recommended for those with high acidity in the stomach). For those who have had their gallbladder removed, an enzyme supplement that includes ox bile is required to be taken to help in the digestion of fats.

Food Combining

The art of food combining has helped many people over the years to break down and digest their food more easily. The idea is that the body has difficulty digesting a carbohydrate and protein at the same time. Allowable food combinations are proteins and non-starchy vegetables, or carbohydrates with non-starchy veggies, but not protein and carbohydrates or starchy vegetables at the same time (See chart below). Fruit is always eaten alone – either twenty minutes before a meal, or two to three hours after. Fruit is digested very quickly, and if it is eaten after a protein or carbohydrate meal, it starts to ferment in the digestive tract, because it has to wait for the other foods to digest. This type of bad food combining can lead to gas and bloating and more seriously, dysbiosis, which I discussed earlier in Chapter One.

NON-STARCHY VEGETABLES	STARCHY VEGETABLES	CARBOHYDRATES	PROTEINS
Lettuce	Beets	Breads	Fish
Broccoli	Carrots	Pasta	Chicken
Cauliflower	Parsnips	Bagels	Beef
Spinach	Potatoes	Baked goods	Turkey
Rapini	Corn	Anything with refined sugar	Lamb
Chard	Yams		Seafood
Bok choy	Sweet potatoes		Pork
Asparagus	Squash		

Water

No diet is complete without adequate amounts of pure, clean, non-toxic water. Water has various properties that need to be considered when making a decision as to which water to drink and when.

Acidity and Alkalinity

- Acidic water is less favourable for health because metabolic processes in the body function best in an alkaline state.
- Neutral pH is seven, above seven is alkaline, and below seven is acidic.
- The blood pH must remain between 7.35 and 7.45 or you will die.
- Most harmful bacteria, viruses and cancer cells thrive in an acidic environment.
- When the body becomes too acidic, it robs the bones of calcium to maintain an alkaline environment.

Charged and Uncharged

- Water must be negatively charged to have a favourable effect on our cells.
- The oxidation reduction potential (ORP) is the measurement of electrons present and energy potential of a fluid.
- The more negative the number, the more energy (reduced) is available in the water.
- The more positive the number, the less energy (oxidized) is available.
- Charged water is structured; meaning it forms water crystals when seen under the microscope.
- Unstructured water does not form crystals and is disordered.

- Unstructured water can become structured and form beautiful crystals, if exposed to classical music and positive energy (Read *The Hidden Messages in Water* by Masaru Emoto).

Water can be structured in the following ways:

- Place water in a clear glass container in direct sunlight for at least twenty minutes
- Add freshly squeezed lemon to water
- Use crystals to energize water
- Talk positively to water before you drink it or pray over it[22]

Good-quality water flushes toxins through the kidneys, as well as the skin. If you perspire as much as you should to eliminate toxins, you need to replenish that lost water. I am often asked what type of water is the best to drink. The following chart lists the pros and cons of different types of drinking water.

TYPE OF WATER	PROS	CONS
Tap water	Inexpensive, readily accessible	Loaded with toxic elements including: chlorine, lead, mercury, bacteria, parasites, benzenes, xeno-estrogens, cesium, fluoride, acid-forming, positively charged
Spring water	Readily accessible, minerals present	Excess inorganic minerals not easily absorbed by the body, may be acid-forming, freshness hard to determine. Bottled waters can harbour bacteria just 2 weeks after being bottled
Filtered • Carbon blocks • Brita • Water pik	Removes volatile organic compounds, some pesticides	Filters collect bacteria and, at any one filling, can dump bacteria into drinking water
Reverse osmosis	Removes heavy metals, arsenic, cost effective convenient once-a-year maintenance to replace filters, water is always available on tap	No minerals in water, making it "hungry water" that leaches minerals from the body, such as calcium and magnesium, water is uncharged, causing increase in white blood cells, lowers immunity
Distilled	Removes lead, radon, salts, metals, sediments, very cost effective, low annual maintenance costs	No minerals (see above), water is uncharged (see above)
Ozonated (California)	Removes bacteria, viruses	Only available in bottled waters, not as a system for drinking water

The formula for calculating how much water you should drink in a day is as follows:

One ounce of water per kilogram of bodyweight per day.
(See Chapter One: Detoxification of the Body; Kidneys).

Water bottles

If you buy bottled water in plastic, you should be aware that the plastic from the bottle can leach into the water. The numbers in the triangular recycling logos represent different types of plastics – some being more harmful than others. Polycarbonate products are identified by #7, and may be harmful, even though they are a hard plastic. They give off a chemical called Bisphenol-A, which is a hormone disruptor.[23] It may be safer to use #5 (polypropylene) or #2 (high-density polyethylene) or #4 (low-density polyethylene). The worst type is #1, which is found in most clear water bottles made from polyethylene terephthalate, and may leach a carcinogenic substance. It is especially detrimental to reuse these clear #1 plastic bottles because the plastic breaks down and bacteria and fungi multiply over time.

The best way to store water is in glass. If you buy and drink water from clear plastic water bottles every day (#1 plastic), your cumulative exposure to these chemicals adds up and can be harmful to your health. This is a type of toxicity that you can control and limit your consumption of. You never know how long the water has been sitting in these soft plastics before you even buy them, thus, adding to the number of toxins leached into the water.

Food Sensitivities

Most people have some food sensitivities, whether they are aware of it or not. Food sensitivity is a broad term defining any adverse reaction to food, including food intolerance and food allergy. Food allergies are any adverse reaction to food in which the immune system is demonstrably involved. In many cases, food allergies involve the development of hives or even a severe anaphylactic reaction. Food intolerance is any adverse reaction to food in which the involvement of the immune system is unproven.

Food sensitivities are the cause of numerous health problems, including attention deficit and hyperactivity disorder, eczema, psoriasis, ulcerative colitis, Crohn's disease, headaches and ear infections. The effects of food sensitivities vary greatly from person to person, and the symptoms a person experiences may vary in intensity and frequency, especially according to the amount of the offending food ingested. Symptoms are typically worse when someone is under stress. Food sensitivities and allergies can be tested using a variety of methods:

Quantum QXCI, SCIO stress analysis

- This analysis is a computer-based testing that uses quantum physics technology to measure the frequency reactivity of an individual.

Electrodermal testing

- Suitable for food sensitivities, it involves holding a metal probe in one hand that is connected to either a computer or a Voll meter. The conductivity of the patient's system is tested as a food is introduced into the path of the electricity and the degree of resistance compared with that when there is no food present (the baseline). Foods that show either a very high or low resistance are indicated as food sensitivities as they disrupt the electromagnetism of the individual.

Applied kinesiology

- This technique for food sensitivities is also known as muscle-testing. Patients hold an arm away from the body and resist against the practitioner's pressure, both holding the food and without the food (the baseline). A difference in strength will indicate if the food reacts well or not with the patient's electromagnetic energy.

Needle testing

- Immunoglobin A – an immune system test. Various foods are introduced through a prick in the skin for reactivity. Used to find food allergies.

Blood tests – Enzyme-linked immunosorbent assay (ELISA)

- Immunoglobin G – an immune system test. Blood is drawn from the patient and passed over samples of foods and checked for reactivity.

Radioallergosorbent test (RAST)

- Blood samples are passed over food samples and checked for antibodies, which indicates that an allergic reaction has taken place.

Food sensitivities often develop after someone eats the same food repetitively for a period of time. In North America, we see many patients with sensitivities to wheat and dairy products. If you look at the typical North American diet, it is laden with wheat and dairy on a daily basis. The body prefers a variety of foods. If we consume the same thing over and over again, even in different forms, not only may we lack essential nutrients – which would come from eating more variety – but also our intestinal cells become sensitive and ultimately damaged by the offending foods. This is one of the reasons that naturopathic doctors often recommend that patients try to avoid wheat and dairy for a short time, to give the digestive system a break, and also introduce the body to alternative grains and dairy substitutes.

CASE study

Richard, a successful multi-millionaire, came to see me with the complaint of irritable bowel syndrome (IBS). He was going through a particularly stressful time with his business. My recommendation to him was to practise deep-breathing exercises to reduce the stress, twenty minutes a day. We also tested his food sensitivities and realized he was sensitive to wheat products. He eliminated wheat from his diet and was diligent with the breathing exercises. Within three weeks, his IBS symptoms disappeared – and his business situation improved as well!

Yes, You Can Still Have Your Treats!

It would be great if we could all eat perfectly. In reality, it is very difficult to avoid the "fun foods" and drinks all the time. I usually recommend that my patients watch what they eat very carefully seventy to eighty per cent of the time, and the rest of the time they can indulge in whatever they want. There are some exceptions, such as people with cancer or autoimmune diseases, where the diet needs to be very clean all the time. I find my patients' compliance is much better when they know they can still have some treats, rather than radically changing their diet and only sticking with it for a couple of weeks and saying it doesn't work or they don't feel any better. I also recommend that my patients detoxify their body at least twice a year. We usually detoxify in spring and fall, as this is when the body supports a detox the best. I usually tailor-make the detox regime to suit each individual patient – with herbal and/or homeopathic remedies and dietary changes.

CHAPTER 3 | EXERCISE

Exercise is absolutely essential for the successful and forthcoming millionaire. Typically, this group will often work long hours. Long hours can translate into a lack of time or energy for exercise. Smart millionaires make exercise a necessity that they would never do without. Exercising the physical body helps to keep the circulatory system strong. Strong circulation helps to feed the brain with the nutrients that it needs to keep the million-dollar ideas flowing!

Do What You Love

Exercise is essential for healthy living. It is not an option, but a necessity. Exercise needs to be fun, or else you won't do it. People who push themselves to work out usually cannot remain committed to it for a lifetime. And exercise is a lifetime event. So, if you think of anything that is going to be with you for that long, you'd better love it! Just as there is no one magic diet for everyone, there is also no one perfect exercise regime for all. Our bodies and metabolic types differ dramatically, so we need to try to match our physique and stamina to the type of exercise that is right for us.

Acid and Alkaline Forming Exercise

The pH of our tissues is in constant flux. If our body fluids become too acidic or go the other way and become too alkaline, our systems re-adjust to maintain the proper pH. Our metabolic processes and enzyme systems work the best when the blood pH is 7.35. When we are too acidic, the potential for bacteria and even cancer cells to multiply is increased. Certain types of exercise are too acid-forming. Examples include running, cycling, aerobics and high-intensity sports. For some people, too much of these exercises may be contraindicated if not balanced with alkaline activities, such as stretching, yoga, Pilates, tai chi, qigong and any gentle exercise.[24]

Stress and the Adrenal Glands

Stress activates the adrenal glands that sit on top of the kidneys. Over-stimulation of the adrenals leads to decreased immunity, fatigue, and some diseases. Exercise can also stress the adrenal glands, especially if it is too strenuous – usually of the acid-forming type mentioned above. When people are exercising to lose weight and doing a lot of high-intensity workouts, they often find it difficult to lose the inches. The reason for this is that the adrenal glands produce hormones to store fat instead of burning it. Ask yourself what you like to do that gets your blood flowing. If it is dancing, then dance more, and dance frequently.

Yoga

Yoga has become increasingly popular over the past decade in North America. There are so many different types of yoga that you really need to try them out to find which one is the best match for you. I particularly enjoy Ashtanga, or Power Yoga. It is strenuous and looks a lot easier than it is. The first time I tried it I couldn't walk properly for three days afterward. So those who think yoga is all about breathing and meditating, this is one to try.

One of the reasons I love yoga so much is that it encompasses the body, mind and spirit. You use the breath to connect the physical postures with the calming of the mind, sedating of the nervous system, and fulfilment of the spirit. Ancient yogis believed that the diaphragm was the seat of intelligence and the window to the soul. Stress causes tightness in the diaphragm that can be relieved through yogic breathing and the postures. When the diaphragm is more elastic and supple, one can handle any stress. Yoga also gives all the internal organs a massage. The breath is used to create space in the ribcage where all the major emunctories, or eliminative organs, are housed. By allowing for more room for these organs and simultaneously breathing in more oxygen, a cleansing occurs without the need of taking any supplements, herbs or homeopathics.

A newer type of yoga is Bikram yoga, Moksha or hot yoga. It is performed in a hot room, usually at forty degrees Celsius, or 105 degrees Fahrenheit and sixty per cent humidity. The basic yoga postures are practised in the intense heat. The heat allows you to stretch further in the poses, and has the added benefit of heavy perspiration. You literally drip sweat and need to stand on a towel over your yoga mat to collect your perspiration. Bikram yoga is probably the best detoxification workout. One of my patients started Bikram and for the first two months her skin burned from her perspiration. She was convinced she was detoxifying some chemicals, which were being released in her sweat. After the first two months, her sweat no longer burned her skin, probably signifying that her system cleared the toxins.

The practice of yoga strengthens the spirit and the body because the "monkey mind" is forced to relax. When the mind is turned off, outside fears that run so many of our toxic thoughts are not able to invade our bodies. The unique advantage to this type of exercise is that it transfers into our daily life, so we can become more productive and focused.

One of the best ways to warm up in yoga is by performing the sun salutation. It is a series of postures that produces heat in the body and warms up all the major muscle groups. The sun salutation can be easily found in many yoga books, websites and videos. I strongly recommend warming up with at least three sun salutations before doing the following detoxification postures.

The following postures are specific for detoxifying the listed organs.[25] Like most other sports and exercises, yoga can be modified to be very difficult and advanced. Usually, the postures remain the same, just a deeper and further stretch makes the level of difficulty higher.

POSTURE	ORGANS AFFECTED	CONTRAINDICATIONS FOR POSTURE
Uttanasana (Standing forward bend)	Calms the mind, massages and detoxifies the liver, spleen and kidneys	Spinal disc disorders, for dizziness, keep legs apart
Utthita Parsvakonasana (Extended side-angle stretch)	Detoxifies the lungs and heart, aids digestion, decreases fat around the waist and hips	High blood pressure, with cervical problems, avoid turning head to look up
Utthita Trikonasana (Extended triangle pose)	Detoxifies the liver, spleen, pancreas, kidneys, massages the pelvis, helps with gastric distress, indigestion, acidity and gas, helps relieve menstrual cramps	High blood pressure, heart conditions
Marichyasana (Spinal twist)	Detoxifies the liver, spleen, pancreas, kidneys and intestines, moves the bowels, massages all the abdominal organs, reduces fat around the waist	Migraine or other headaches, diarrhea, fatigue, menstruation

UTTANASANA
(Standing forward bend)
Stand with feet hip-width apart. As you exhale, bend forward from the waist. Lengthen the spine and keep the neck long. Let your arms hang loosely, reaching down only as far as they will go naturally. You can increase the stretch by pulling from your heels, up the back of your legs

and spine to bend further. Relax the neck and the shoulders. Pull the belly in as you breathe deeply. When you are ready, come up slowly, exhaling, keeping your feet planted firmly to the ground.

UTTHITA PARSVAKONASANA
(Extended side-angle stretch)

With the right foot forward and pointing away from the right side of your body, the left foot anchors your weight and lines up its arch with the heel of the right foot. Arms are extended to the sides, shoulders down and relaxed. Stance can be with legs one foot to three feet apart, depending on your flexibility. Stick the left hip out and bend slowly towards your right leg as you exhale. Most of the weight is in your right foot. Keep the spine straight, parallel to the floor. The hand can be placed as far down as possible, either beside the knee, lower leg, on the foot or on the floor. Head can be turned to look forward, or for the advanced, look up at the hand. Pull the belly in and breathe. To finish the posture, exhale and come up to standing. Repeat on the other side.

UTTHITA TRIKONASANA
(Triangle pose)

Turn the right foot out forty-five degrees and the arch of the left foot lines up with the heel of the right foot. Feet should be about two feet apart. Arms are extended to the sides. Stick the left hip out to the left and exhaling, bend from the waist to the right side. Right arm can rest on the knee, lower leg or floor. Keep the weight evenly distributed between the feet with a slight emphasis on the right leg. Turn the head to either look down at the floor, straight ahead or up to your left hand. Keep the shoulders relaxed and down. With the belly pulled in, breathe. When you are ready to come out of the posture, look down and pull yourself up using your core muscles with the belly in, exhaling. Repeat on the other side.

MARICHYASANA
(Spinal twist)

Sit with both legs in front of you. Make sure you are on your sitting bones with weight evenly distributed. Bend your right leg, placing your right foot on the floor, as close to your right sitting bone as possible. Twist your body to the right side. The right hand stabilizes your weight behind your right buttock. The left hand and arm is bent and goes to the outside of your right leg. If this is too much of a stretch, keep the left arm on top of the right knee. Breathe deeply, with the belly in, making sure the weight is in both sitting bones. Release the arms. Straighten the legs. Repeat on the other side.[26]

Pilates

Joseph Pilates was born in Germany in 1880. He was not well as a child and developed a method of strengthening and elongating the muscles to improve his own physique. He combined both Eastern and Western exercises, such as yoga, gymnastics and diving. He also watched animals in the wild and simulated moves and stretches that they did to help to rehabilitate injured humans.

Pilates is a great exercise for strengthening the core muscles of the body. It helps to elongate the spine and correct posture, tone muscles and increase mobility in joints, like no other exercise I have ever tried. Pilates is loved by dancers and helps to achieve and maintain a dancer's body streamlined and strong.

Pilates classes are usually of two types: either mat classes, or classes using the special Pilates machines. Many health clubs and fitness centres are now starting to offer Pilates classes because they have seen the benefits for their clients. You can also purchase Pilates workout DVDs to practise at home. To see results quickly, it is best to do it at least three times a week, for one half to one hour each time.

Weight Training

Weight training is an important part of any fitness regime. The lifting of weights helps to maintain lean muscle mass; it tones and strengthens muscles needed for everyday activities; it helps to maintain a healthy body weight; and it strengthens the bones. I believe that free weights offer the best benefits, however, it is very important that you use the proper form when training. Now fitness clubs are introducing aerobic-type classes that are just for lifting weights. I do them regularly and love the motivation of the music and having an instructor's guidance through the exercises. Check your local gym to see if they offer this type of class. Weight training can be monotonous, so this type of class alleviates the boredom and forces you to work hard.

Cardiovascular Exercise

Cardiovascular training is a must for keeping the heart and lungs healthy. I usually suggest that, no matter what type of cardio you are doing, you work your way up to a sweat and stay there for at least twenty minutes. Perspiration during exercise is one of the only ways to mobilize toxins in fat cells to be detoxified by the emunctories, or detox organs.

Cardio training helps to burn off unwanted body fat, especially when combined with a weight-lifting routine. Cardiovascular exercise also helps the mind, in that chemicals called endorphins are released to give you that "runner's high."

Cardiovascular exercise should be aerobic, which means "with oxygen." Oxygen is required to burn fat. A good way to measure if you are working aerobically is to try to talk while exercising. If you can talk comfortably, you are in the aerobic zone. If you are winded and can't speak, you are working anaerobically – and burning more glycogen than fat.

It is important that you do a warm-up and cool-down before and after each cardio session. This ensures that little stress is placed on the heart and lungs during exercise, and that your blood is gradually distributed to the areas that need it, such as the arms and legs.

Sweat

Perspiration allows the pores of the skin to open and flushes toxins out. I have heard countless stories from people at the gym who work out hard and sweat buckets when they are sick, to rid themselves of the toxins in their systems. They always report feeling better the next day. The same is true for using saunas and steam rooms for the same purpose. The Europeans have taken advantage of saunas and steam rooms for years. One of the only ways to mobilize toxins stored in fat cells is to perspire them out.

Exercise should always be at the level of intensity that induces sweating, and then staying at that level for at least twenty minutes. It is very important to have a shower right after sweating to wash away the toxins. If you do not at least wipe your sweat away after exercise, the toxins are reabsorbed into the body. Make sure you wash your workout clothes really well for this reason. It may be wise to use the extra-rinse cycle on your washing machine for your workout clothes.

Frequency of Exercise

Exercise should be a daily event. If you think back to a time when there were no cars, tractors or appliances, people were much more active than we are today. We have become lazy, and our bodies show it. I usually recommend intense exercise three times a week, with more moderate forms of exercise on the days in between.

It is important to vary exercise routines. The body begins to adapt to the exercise style it is used to, and results will be minimal, if the same type of exercise is repeated.

Water

Be sure to consume enough water during exercise. It is better to sip small amounts of water throughout your workout, rather than gulping down a lot all at once. Your body only absorbs close to two ounces of water at once. If you consume more than this at any one time, it is filtered directly through the kidneys and urinated out.

Breathing During Exercise

Breathing during exercise is also a form of detoxification through the lungs. When weight training, you should breathe in on relaxation of the muscle and exhale on exertion. It is also important to be breathing fresh air while exercising, or else the positive detoxification benefits will be outweighed by pollution.

Oxygen is required to burn fat during exercise. If you breathe effectively during your workouts, you can burn body fat more quickly. This is one of the reasons why I love yoga. The whole practice of yoga is centred on the breath. The more deeply you breathe in each of the postures, the more beneficial it is to the detoxification of the organs that are targeted.

Rest and Recovery

Your muscles grow when you are resting. Rest is essential for secreting growth hormone, which is most prevalent in the bloodstream during sleep. Growth hormone helps to repair damaged tissue, which stimulates the growth of muscle cells. Listening to your body is essential when exercising regularly. If your body needs to rest, then let it rest. The more intuitive you become, the easier it will be to follow an exercise regime that changes in activity and length of time as often as your individual body changes in its biorhythms and life cycles.

Intuitive Exercise

Intuitive exercise means following your body's wisdom in what it needs for exercise on any given day. Because our systems change from day to day, the type and length of time we can sustain exercise on any given day changes as well. If we can learn to listen to what our body needs, we can provide it with the best set of exercises to keep us healthy and strong. You need to push yourself just past the point where you think you are capable of going when exercising. For example, if you are running on a treadmill for ten minutes and feel that's all you can do, try to go a bit longer to get the full benefit of the exercise – keeping in mind not to go to the point of exhaustion or heart failure!

Ayurvedic Exercise Types

Everybody has a different composition and tolerance for various types of exercise. For instance, the Indian Ayurvedic medical principles divide people into three categories or doshas: vata, pitta or kapha. Everyone has characteristics of all three doshas, but generally one dosha is the dominant constitution. The following chart[27] emphasizes characteristics of each body type, and which exercises benefit each type to its fullest potential. Keep in mind that you may fall in-between two (or even all three) of the categories, thus, making it easier for you to choose any exercise, as they all suit you well.

DOSHA	CHARACTERISTICS	EXERCISES
Vata	Air element, either very tall or very short, weight can fluctuate, but mainly thin, anxious, overachievers	Vata people love vigorous exercise, but it is best to balance this dosha with regular gentle exercise, such as yoga or Pilates
Pitta	Fire element, fair skin, well-proportioned body, freckles/red hair, fiery personality, impulsive, weight is steady, easily burned out, competitive	Cooling sports, such as swimming and skiing, are helpful to balance the fire in this dosha Pitta personalities should avoid competitive sports as they are inherently competitive enough
Kapha	Water element, larger build, tend to be mucousy, phlegmatic, slow, heavy physically and psychologically	Vigorous exercise helps kapha types to create more heat and burn off the excess water and should be done frequently for long periods of time Long walks, bike rides or jogging are helpful for kapha individuals

Chinese Medicine Approach to Exercise

As the seasons change, so should the type of exercise, according to Chinese medicine. In the spring, with the arrival of more sunlight, we tend to have more energy and motivation and can begin to do more strenuous exercise, such as jogging, cycling and aerobics. In the wintertime, however, it is best to conserve our energy and kidney essence. It is best to do lower key exercises – yoga and tai chi – in the colder months. The cold also weakens the heart, so it is advisable to not overtax the heart with rigorous exercise in the winter.[28]

Athletic Supplements: Do They Really Help?

Protein Powder

There are a variety of protein powders on the market today. Most are either whey-based or from soy. I tend to recommend the soy formulas more often than whey because most people digest soy better than dairy-based formulas. Protein is essential in the production of lean muscle mass. Protein deficiency and carbohydrate overload can lead to obesity.

The standard adult dose for protein powder to gain muscle mass and increase fat loss is one protein shake per day during a treatment period, with ten to twenty grams of protein per shake.

Banana Soy Shake

1 scoop plain, vanilla or chocolate soy protein powder
1/2 to 1 banana
1 1/2 cups soy milk (plain, vanilla or chocolate)
1/2 tsp pure vanilla extract
3 ice cubes

Blend thoroughly in blender.

Essential fatty acids

Athletes used to stay clear of all fats, thinking that they would pack on weight if they were included in the diet. However, modern advances in nutritional biochemistry have made fats popular again. The importance of essential fatty acid for athletes, and those who want to lose weight, lies in the fact that they help to make cells more efficient at burning unwanted body fat. Essential fats also help to satiate, or make us feel full more quickly. For this reason, we end up eating fewer calories and can go longer without eating. Essential fats also help to maintain blood sugar levels, so that we stay fuller longer.

CHAPTER 4 | ENVIRONMENTAL TOXICITY

We are exposed to a number of environmental toxins every day, the dangers of many of which we are not even aware of. The most toxic exposure we have is in our own homes. The building materials, carpets, paint, flooring, countertops, furniture, cleaning products and mattresses are some of the sources of our daily exposure to toxins, which we don't even think of as noxious substances. We may not be able to change many of these sources of pollution in our homes, but, at the very least, we can ensure fresh air and possibly an air filtration system to help to minimize the toxic gases and chemicals in the air.

Toxins in Our Homes

The following is a list of sources of chemical exposure in the home and possible solutions or alternatives that are less toxic.

SOURCE OF TOXINS	CHEMICALS EMITTED	ALTERNATIVES
Building materials, pressed wood, fibreboard, plywood, particle board	Formaldehyde	Untreated wood
Carpets	Volatile organic compounds (VOCs), lead, animal dander, pesticides	Hardwood flooring without formaldehyde
Hardwood flooring	Formaldehyde	Untreated wood
Paint	VOCs	Latex is better than oil-based paint for fumes
Countertops	Formaldehyde	Stone or marble
Cleaning supplies	Chlorine	Vinegar, natural cleaning products available at health food stores, Eco Mist Solutions
Mattresses	Mould, dust mites	Vacuum mattress for 20 minutes, every few months, use anti-mite mattress covers
Pillows	Dust mites	Change pillows every few years, wash pillowcase once a week, use anti-mite pillow covers
Microwaves	Microwave radiation	Use oven/toaster oven instead
Computers	Electromagnetic emissions	Use protectors/shields for electromagnetic energy

SOURCE OF TOXINS	CHEMICALS EMITTED	ALTERNATIVES
Televisions	Electromagnetic emissions	Buy plasma screens, sit at least 6 feet from screen, only turn on when watching
Tobacco smoke	Carbon monoxide, nitrogen dioxide, formaldehyde	Stop smoking, avoid exposure to second-hand smoke
Pesticides	A variety of toxic chemicals	Wash with Veggie Wash, buy organic whenever possible, grow your own without chemicals
Chimney, furnaces, woodstoves	Radon, carbon monoxide	Ventilate well

Formaldehyde
Formaldehyde is found in the glues used to install carpets in the home, countertops, drapery, particleboard, cabinets and cigarette smoke.

Symptoms of toxicity:
- Eye, nose and throat irritation
- Wheezing
- Cough
- Fatigue
- Skin rash
- Severe allergic reaction
- May be linked to cancer

Solutions for decreasing toxicity:
- Decrease humidity in home, which decreases out-gassing of formaldehyde
- Increase ventilation
- Use plants that capture formaldehyde, such as spider plants, philodendron and golden pothos.

Pesticides
Pesticides, insecticides and termiticides from outdoor plants and lawns can be tracked into our homes on our shoes.

Symptoms of toxicity:
- Eye, nose and throat irritation
- Damage to central nervous system
- Kidney damage
- Increased risk of cancer

Solutions for decreasing toxicity:

- Avoid using chemical pesticides
- Find natural alternatives for killing weeds
- Do not store these chemical compounds in the house
- Remove shoes at home

Dust Mites

Dust mites are microscopic creatures from the arachnid family, which includes spiders, scorpions and ticks. They live in pillows, mattresses, carpets, furniture and clothing. They feed off of our dead skin cells and their droppings are usually a cause for allergic reactions.

These are some of the symptoms of sensitivity to dust mites:

- Year-round allergies
- Asthma
- Breathing difficulties
- Rashes, eczema
- Chronic nasal irritation and discharge

Solutions for decreasing toxicity:

- Wash bedsheets at least once a week at a minimum temperature of 140°F or 56°C
- Wash sheets with Citricidal (grapefruit seed extract) ten drops in washing machine
- After sleeping in sheets, do not make bed right away; let sheets dry out from body heat and perspiration for at least two hours
- Use non-allergenic pillows and comforters instead of down
- Use dust mite-reducing pillow covers and mattress covers
- Air bedclothes outside in direct sunlight
- Place pillow in large plastic bag and hold vacuum hose inside bag to form a seal and suction out all mites and dead skin cells
- Air filtration system, especially in bedroom
- Air out bedroom for twenty minutes, twice a day
- Keep humidity relatively low in house, not higher than seventy per cent
- Use vacuum cleaner with HEPA filter
- Vacuum mattress thoroughly four times a year
- Avoid carpeting
- No stuffed animals in children's rooms

Mould

Mould consists of tiny spores that come into the house in the air, on surfaces of fruits and vegetables, clothing, furniture and pets. The most common types of moulds in homes and offices include penicillium, aspergillus, cladosporium and stachybotrys. Moulds grow in dark, moist environments. In the home, moulds are commonly found on window sills (the fuzzy black residue), in refrigerators, shower stalls, bathrooms, under carpets (especially after steam cleaning) and basements.

There have been over 270 different species of moulds found in Canadian homes. They can be any colour and they release chemicals and spores into neighbouring air, which are toxic.

Symptoms of toxicity:
- Allergic reactions
- Asthma
- Eczema
- Chronic upper respiratory tract infections
- Sinusitis
- Candida (See Chapter Six: Candidiasis; Symptoms of Candidia)

Solutions for decreasing toxicity:
- Control moisture levels in the home
- Do not carpet wet areas such as bathrooms
- Clean fridge once a month with Citricidal/water solution (fifteen drops Citricidal to one litre water in a spray bottle)
- After a flood, replace what can't be thoroughly cleaned and dried out.

CASE study

A patient that I had been seeing for a couple of years with fungus on the soles of her feet brought her daughter and son in for me to take a look at their skin. The daughter, aged five, had a rash on her abdomen that looked much like ringworm, a fungal infection. The son, aged two, had rough scaly skin on the soles of his feet and what looked like the beginnings of athlete's foot. The children's skin problems had only started in the previous few weeks. I asked what had changed and if there was a mould or fungus problem in the house. Sure enough, the family had just moved and their refrigerator was in storage for a few months during their move and had not been disinfected before use again in the new house. (Fridges are a common breeding ground for fungi and their spores that end up on the food we eat). The new house had been inspected and treated for a mould problem before they moved in. Once these environmental mould issues were cleaned up in the house and the family took remedies to clear the physical symptoms of mould, the fungus problems disappeared.

Lead

Lead sources include lead in paint manufactured before 1978, lead pipes, pipes with lead solder, enamelled and ceramic pots, children's costume jewellery and toys, candy bar wrappers, fertilizers, fungicides, water heaters and anti-lock braking systems in cars.

Symptoms of toxicity:

- Nausea, vomiting, diarrhea, gastro-intestinal pain
- Sluggishness
- Developmental disorders
- Abortion
- High blood pressure
- Kidney toxicity
- Blood cell irregularities
- Discoloured lips, lead line in gums

Solutions for decreasing toxicity:

- Check water for lead contamination
- Check soil surrounding house
- If lead paint is in an older home, have it professionally removed, because when it is sanded and stripped, lead contamination increases in the environment.

Carbon Monoxide

Carbon monoxide is very dangerous because it cannot be detected by any of our five senses. It is an invisible, odourless and tasteless gas that is commonly found in homes. Its sources include leaking chimneys, furnaces, woodstoves, exhaust from cars parked in adjoining garages, gas water-heaters and tobacco smoke.

Symptoms of toxicity:

- Fatigue
- Chest pain in people with pre-existing heart disease
- Impaired vision and coordination
- Headaches
- Dizziness
- Confusion
- Nausea
- Flu-like symptoms

Solutions for detoxification:

- Monitor levels with a carbon monoxide detector in basement and bedrooms
- Ensure proper venting to outside
- Do not let car idle in garage

Radon

Radon is a radioactive element that cannot be smelled, tasted or seen. It is produced by the breakdown of uranium in soil, rock and water beneath homes. It is also found in well water and building materials. Radon emits alpha particles when it breaks down that directly affect lung tissue. Radon is the second leading cause of lung cancer in the U.S. Radon leaks into homes through cracks in basement floors and walls, and concrete block walls. Also, it is prevalent in some water wells. In Canada, fewer than a tenth of homes have levels that are higher than acceptable as deemed by Health Canada.

Radon can be tested with charcoal canisters and alpha track detectors that are available in hardware stores in the U.S. The results are sent to laboratories that measure the levels of radon.

Symptoms of toxicity:

- Lung pathologies
- Emphysema
- Pulmonary fibrosis
- Chronic interstitial pneumonia
- Lung cancer

Solutions for decreasing toxicity:

- Seal all cracks in basement floors, walls, around pipes and drains
- Improve ventilation in basement

Cleaning Products

I always question my patients about any toxic exposure they may have had over their lifetime. In most cases, they do not recall a single event that may have increased their toxic load. However, when I ask what they use, or their help uses for home cleaning products, they look at me with big eyes and say, "Oh! Of course, all the toxic ones!" Most people know that what they are using can't be that good for them, but they figure as long as they don't ingest them, they are fine. Wrong. The skin and respiratory tracts are great entry routes for these toxins into the body, where they can wreak havoc.

The chart on the next page explores some of the most common toxins in home cleaning products.[29]

PRODUCT	CHEMICALS	HEALTH EFFECTS
Toilet bowl cleaners	Hydrochloric bleach	Fumes are irritant to eyes, skin absorption toxic, respiratory toxins, liver, heart toxicity
Carpet cleaners	Ammonium hydroxide	Corrosive to skin, fumes cause long-term eye and lung damage
	Perchlorethylene	Carcinogenic, toxic to liver, kidneys and central nervous system
Cleaners and detergents	Ammonia	Highly volatile, eye, skin, lung toxicity
	Ammonium hydroxide	Corrosive, lung, eye and skin irritant
	Bleach	Burns eyes, skin and lungs, heart, liver, GI toxicity
	Butyl	Suspected carcinogen, eye, lung and skin toxicity
	Diethylene glycol	Central nervous system irritant, liver, kidney toxicity
	Formaldehyde	Highly toxic carcinogen, present in most carpet, fabrics and colouring
	Isopropanol	Carcinogen, toxic to lungs, nervous system, distorts DNA
	Petroleum solvents	Skin, eyes, nose, throat, lung toxicity, causes skin cancer
	Potassium hydroxide	Burns eyes and skin, fumes toxic to respiratory tract
	Sodium hypochlorite	Highly toxic, burns eyes and skin, causes lung edema, coma and death
	Trichloroethane	Toxic to liver, kidneys and central nervous system
	Triclosan	Easily absorbed via skin, causes liver damage
Degreasers	Petroleum solvents	High fire danger, irritates skin, eyes, throat and lungs, linked to skin and lung cancer
Dishwasher detergents	Chlorine	Common cause of childhood deaths due to poisoning
	Diethanolsamine	Burns skin and eyes
	Naphtha	Liver toxicity
Disinfectants	Bleach	Burns eyes, skin and lungs
	Cresol	Liver, spleen, pancreas and central nervous system toxicity
	Phenylphenol	Eye irritant, may cause vision loss
Drain cleaners	Hydrochloric acid	Liver, kidney, lung, skin and eye toxicity
	Trichloroethane	Liver, kidney, central nervous system toxicity
Furniture polish	Diethylene glycol	Fumes harm central nervous system, liver and kidneys
	Petroleum distillates	Carcinogenic, linked to lung and skin cancer
	Phenol	Causes cold sweats, convulsions, circulatory collapse, coma and death
Glass cleaners	Ammonia	Fumes toxic to eyes, skin and lungs
	Diethylene glycol	Fumes toxic to central nervous system, liver and kidneys

Safe, environmentally friendly cleaning products

Thankfully, a new generation of completely organic, non-toxic and environmentally friendly cleaning products is available. Based on colloidal nanotechnology, these products are better than any other I have ever used before. They work even better than the toxic ones! The company is called Eco Mist Solutions. I will describe the way they work to the best of my ability, however the technology is advanced and a bit complicated to wrap your head around.

Nano/Colloidal Chemistry

More than fifty years ago, colloidal chemistry was discovered by David Graham, a British chemist. The basis of this chemistry is the formation of a colloidal micelle. This micelle is about the size of ten hydrogen atoms, or one nanometre. Sub-microscopic particles are created in a microscopic field similar to a magnetic field.

These micelles are created as a result of a process in which extracts of natural plants and food additives are blended at specific time intervals, temperatures and sequences. Colloidal micelles are then miraculously formed from the original organic compounds. An attraction of like poles occurs, differing greatly from traditional chemistry in which positive and negative attract. In the case of colloidal micelles, negative attracts negative and positive attracts positive. One pole of the micelle attracts water particles (hydrophilic) and the other side of the micelle repels water (hydrophobic). The water- repelling molecules join together, forming the inside of the micelle, and the water-attracting molecules form the outside of the micelle.

When the micelle then comes into contact with a hydrocarbon (oily stain), it is able to disrupt its attraction to the surface to which it is attached (carpet, sink, toilet). The number of micelles used to clean is in the billions. The oily stain is then magically emulsified and clears away easily with water. Eco Mist also kills bacteria, viruses, fungus and insects. It will soon become a natural insecticide and fungicide used in agriculture around the world.

The environmental saving aspect that is so beneficial about the product is that it does not cause toxic run off into the ground water. Biological oxygen demand is then reduced, leaving oxygen for the fish and aquatic ecosystems. From a parent's perspective, if your kids get their hands on it and drink it, you need not be worried as you do for all the other toxic home cleaners. It is made from organic food-grade products. I'm not advising that you drink it, but if you did it wouldn't kill you.

Eco Mist products can be used to clean just about everything, including:

- Automobiles
- Glass, mirrors
- Pots and pans
- Ovens
- Barbeques
- Sinks
- Toilets
- Countertops
- Floors
- Hardwood
- Jet engines
- Clothes
- Fridge
- Stovetop
- Carpets
- Food preparation facilities
- Garbage cans
- Fryers, grease traps
- Concrete floors
- Grout
- Coffee makers
- Upholstery

And much more!

For more information, visit www.ecomistsolutions.com

Air Filtration

Air filtration systems can be helpful to decrease the amount of dust and airborne toxins in your home or office. The following are standard characteristics you should look for in air filtration systems:

HEPA (high-efficiency particulate arrestance) filters remove as small as 3% micron particles at 99.97% efficiency

- Trapped particles stay attached and never flush out of the filter
- No by-products such as ozone are created by filtration
- True HEPA filters need to be certified

Electrostatically charged fibres (electret-type)

- Particles are electrostatically attracted to the filter fibres
- Efficiency decreases with time as fibres become dirty

Electrostatic precipitator

- Particles are charged and then attach to metal plates, which have the opposite electrical charge to attract them
- Efficiency decreases with time as the metal plates become dirty
- Can generate ozone as a by-product, which is not healthy

Ionizer

- High voltage negatively charges airborne particles
- If unit is only an ionizer, the particles are not trapped and just released into the air once charged
- Once in the air, the charged particles attach to surfaces of objects in the room
- Charged particles may be more harmful to the lungs when inhaled

Plants That Clean the Air

Plants can clean the air of unwanted chemical gases, such as formaldehyde, benzene and carbon monoxide.

The following is a list from a NASA study of the top 10 plants to clear these toxins[30]:

1.	Bamboo palm	*Chamaedorea seifritzii*
2.	Chinese evergreen	*Aglaonema Modestum*
3.	English ivy	*Hedera Helix*
4.	Gerbera daisy	*Gerbera Jamesonii*
5.	Janet Craig	*Dracena "Janet Craig"*
6.	Marginata	*Dracena Marginata*
7.	Mass cane/ corn plant	*Dracena Massangeana*
8.	Mother-in-law's tongue	*Sansevieria Laurentii*
9.	Pot mum	*Chrysantheium morifolium*
10.	Peace lwily	*Spathiphyllum "Mauna Loa"*
11.	Warneckii	*Dracaena "Warneckii"*

Education

The more you know, the less likely you will choose the more toxic alternative when you have the choice. There is a website set up by the U.S. National Institutes of Health, which lists common household products, their ingredients, and the toxicity of these ingredients.

CHAPTER 5 | HEAVY METAL TOXICITY

A heavy metal is any metallic chemical element that has a high density and is toxic, even at low concentrations. The problem with heavy metals is their ability to bioaccumulate. Bioaccumulation means the metals do not leave the body on their own accord easily and can accumulate in certain tissues for years. The metals will not be cleared by the system unless some type of intervention is used to chelate (bind and eliminate) the metals and flush them out. There are some metal toxic entities that are more prevalent than others, such as mercury from dental fillings and lead, from lead pipes and paint. Unfortunately, heavy metals have a negative impact on overall health and well-being. They suppress the immune system and can lead to chronic yeast and candida problems (Described in Chapter Six: Candidiasis and Fungal Infections).

Avoidance of heavy metals through education is the best medicine. However, if you have been exposed, different forms of chelation therapy are available to detoxify these compounds.

Mercury

Mercury toxicity is rampant today from the induction of mercury metal amalgams for dental fillings. Unfortunately, some dentists still use mercury fillings for their patients, as they are taught the amalgams that are fifty per cent mercury are safe. Even Health Canada states that even though "dental amalgam is the single largest source of mercury exposure for average Canadians, current evidence does not indicate that dental amalgam is causing illness in the general population." They go on to say, "There is a small percentage of the population which is hypersensitive to mercury and can suffer severe health effects from even a low exposure." So, my first question would be, do dentists even check for mercury sensitivity before using an amalgam? And, if so, how is it tested?

Sources of Mercury

Health Canada also advises that pregnant women do not have amalgams removed or placed. Mercury crosses the placenta and affects the unborn child. For this reason, even if you do not have any mercury amalgams, you may have mercury toxicity from exposure through your mother. You should also take care that if you are pregnant and having a regular dental cleaning or check-up, you are not in the dental office at the same time as another patient who is having their mercury amalgams either removed or placed. When the dentist drills into an existing amalgam, mercury vapour is released into the air and can easily be inhaled by those nearby.

Other sources for mercury toxicity to be aware of:
Fish – especially larger fish that live longer and bioaccumulate more mercury, such as tuna, swordfish, mackerel, shark, salmon, large bass, pike, trout, halibut and snapper
Shellfish – particularly shrimp
Latex paints
Fungicides, pesticides
Cosmetics
Thermometers
Vapours from sewage treatment plants
Batteries
Fluorescent lights; energy efficient light bulbs
Petroleum products
Vaccines (see note on next page)

> Vaccinations are NOT MANDATORY! Contrary to popular belief, your children do not need to be vaccinated to attend school. You merely need to have a form notarized that states your request to have your child omitted from any vaccination protocol. In Canada, this form can be obtained online at www.vran.org

Thimerosal is a preservative in many childhood vaccines that is forty-nine point five per cent ethyl mercury by weight. Mercury is toxic, especially to infants and young children. Studies are now showing a link between autism and thimerosal exposure in children who have difficulty with the mercury. The Environmental Protection Agency in the U.S. allows 10 mcg of mercury per kg body weight per day. The FDA also stated that a safe dose was on a daily basis. However, in the first six months of an infant's life, the doses of thimerosal in vaccines are concentrated in three vaccines on three days. The standard vaccination schedule can expose an infant to as much as 125 times the EPA's allowable level for mercury.[31]

Unfortunately, the issue of vaccination is very controversial. What is even more alarming is that most people and unsuspecting parents do not even know of the controversy and risks that surround vaccination.

Symptoms of Mercury Toxicity:
Abdominal pain, vomiting, diarrhea, bloody stools, fatigue, headache, insomnia, nervousness, impaired judgment and coordination, loss of libido, emotional instability, hypothyroidism, foggy thinking, chronic fungal infection and candidiasis. Mercury injures cell membranes, inactivates enzymes, interferes with protein structure of cells, and decreases the function of Peyer's patches in the gut, which leads to decreased immunity. It also decreases thyroid function because it binds selenium, which is an essential co-factor of thyroid function.

Lead

Lead is the fifth most used metal in the U.S. and is most detrimental to children. Lead causes brain damage in children exposed to high levels. Prenatal exposure may cause birth defects, miscarriage and underdeveloped babies.

Sources of Lead

- Children's costume jewellery
- Fishing tackle
- Food
- Water pipes
- Lead-based paint
- Tin cans, in the solder that binds them together
- Glazed earthenware
- Pesticides
- Ammunition
- Brass
- Cigarette smoke
- Cosmetics

Lead damages the kidneys, brain, blood (it enters the red blood cells), muscles and bones.

Symptoms of Lead Toxicity

Chronic kidney disease, hypertension, encephalopathy, anemia, gout, sterility, abortion, fatigue, irritability, attention deficit disorder (ADD), hyperactivity, memory loss, decreased sensory and motor reaction times, and abdominal pain.

Aluminum

Aluminium is the third most abundant element in the Earth's crust.

Aluminium Sources:

- Food additives
- Antacids
- Buffered aspirin
- Hemorrhoid medication
- Vaccines
- Toothpaste
- Antiperspirants
- Bleaching agents
- Pots
- Tin foil
- Municipal water
- Acid rain
- Dental cements
- Dentures

Aluminum damages the brain (Alzheimer's disease), muscles, liver, lungs, kidneys, skin, reproductive organs, stomach, thyroid and bone.

Symptoms of Aluminium Toxicity:
Constipation, anorexia, gastrointestinal irritation, hyperactivity, speech disorders, dementia, osteomalacia, excessive headaches, abnormal heart rhythm, numbness of hands and feet, blurred vision, and impaired memory.

Aluminum disrupts calcium regulation in the body and also binds phosphorus and iron in the gastrointestinal tract.

Barium
Sources of barium include the following:

- Agent swallowed by patients for certain X-ray procedures
- Ceramics
- Plastics
- Glass
- Picture tubes
- Soap
- Rubber
- Pesticides

Symtoms of Barium Toxicity
Barium displaces potassium in cells, which can lead to muscle weakness, changes in nervous system function and heart abnormalities.

Antimony

Antimony exposure can arise from these sources:

- Flame-resistant clothing, especially children's sleepwear
- Pottery glaze
- Cooking utensils

Cadmium

Cadmium can come from the following sources:

- Air pollution
- Batteries
- Ceramic glazes and enamels
- Cigarette smoke
- Tap water
- Well water
- Food (from soil contamination)
- Paints
- Seafood
- Power and smelting plants
- Fungicides

Cadmium is especially harmful because it increases the permeability of cells allowing other heavy metals to leak into the cells.

Copper

Copper affects the liver, bone marrow, kidneys, spleen, heart, lungs, stomach, intestines, hair, brain and eyes.

Sources of Copper:

- Oysters
- Copper pots
- Water pipes
- Copper bracelets
- Dialysis
- Dental amalgams
- Electric wiring
- Sewage treatment plants
- Braces
- Fungicides
- Algaecides
- Coins
- Supplements

Symptoms of Copper Toxicity

Symptoms of copper toxicity can include abdominal complaints, metallic taste in mouth, schizophrenia, manic depression, learning disabilities, anxiety, depression, hypochondria, poor memory, irritability, fatigue and demyelination of nerves.

Copper is often found in dietary supplements and multivitamins/minerals. One with copper toxicity should never take more copper from an outside source. Copper competes with zinc for absorption, so often the treatment of choice is to supplement zinc.

Laboratory Tests for Heavy Metals

Hair analysis is one way of determining the presence of heavy metals in the body. Heavy metals are excreted in the hair. Hair samples (either from the head or pubic area) are taken and sent to a special lab that processes the results for heavy metal toxicity. The metals usually tested for include aluminum, antimony, arsenic, barium, beryllium, bismuth, cadmium, lead, mercury, copper and silver.

Stool samples can also detect excretion of heavy metals. Pre and post-chelation samples of stool are a good indication of how much metal is being voided by the body.

Naturopathic Detoxification of Heavy Metals

Naturopathy offers some solutions to detoxify heavy metals from the body, namely chelation therapy.

a) **Open the emunctories**

Chelation therapy is the binding and removal of heavy metals from the body. In order to chelate safely, the emunctories, or eliminative organs, need to be working properly, or "open" to receive, then eliminate heavy metal toxins. The organs of excretion need to be functioning optimally when you start to chelate, or remove heavy metals from the body. If the organs do not detoxify as efficiently as they can during the metal detoxification process, there is a danger of becoming more toxic and experiencing more symptoms of toxicity. Your naturopathic doctor will advise you on a specific detoxification protocol for your case.

b) **Remove the source**

The source of toxins needs to be removed as described below, to reduce further exposure to heavy metals.

Mercury dental fillings

The source of heavy metal toxicity should be removed whenever possible before chelation is carried out. This is especially true for mercury amalgam fillings, which are composed of fifty per cent mercury. **It is not recommended to do any detoxification of metals until all the mercury is removed from the mouth.** The danger in leaving in some mercury is that it will begin to leach metal into the mouth with the chelation, leading to further intoxication.

It is important to find the right dentist to carry out the procedure of amalgam removal. Each dentist differs in their protocol for removal. I usually recommend that patients see a dentist that has special training in holistic dentistry or who is a "biological" dentist. It is important to evaluate the patient's toxicity status before and after amalgam removal. The standard practice for removal is one quadrant of the mouth per visit. For instance, all the amalgams from the upper left side of the mouth would be removed in one office visit. For those who are extremely toxic, this may be far too much to be removed at once. It may be advised in such a case that the patient have more visits, only removing one amalgam at a time.

The recommended requirements for safe removal of amalgams in Canada and the U.S. is as follows:

1. Coldwater spray should be used over the amalgams being removed – higher temperatures increase the gassing off of mercury vapour.
2. High-volume suction should be used to evacuate the mercury vapour during drilling.
3. Alternative breathing source should be provided for the patient. The patient should avoid breathing through the mouth during removal, to decrease amount of inhaled mercury vapour. Either air from outside or oxygen can be used as the alternative air source.
4. A rubber dam can be used if the patient's mouth is thoroughly rinsed and suctioned after its removal as mercury can get stuck under the dam.
5. Fillings should be sectioned and removed in large pieces to decrease exposure.
6. Dentist should remove and change gloves and use a new rubber dam before placing new fillings.

7. Room ionizers are available to trap mercury vapour. Ionizers negatively charge the mercury vapour to be collected on a positively charged metal plate.[32]

Aside from dental amalgams as a source for heavy metal toxicity, other sources must also be removed. For example, if you consume a lot of fish that is known to be high in heavy metals, these should be removed from the diet totally. These are the most toxic fish:

- Shark
- Swordfish
- Tuna
- Some salmon
- Mackerel

Intravenous chelation therapy

Intravenous chelation therapy involves the use of compounds, which are injected into a vein, to chelate heavy metals. The most commonly used chelation agents are vitamin C, DMPS and DMSA.

Oral chelation therapy using minerals and nutrients

The following minerals and nutrients have been proven effective at removing heavy metals when taken in supplement form:

- L-Cysteine
- L-Lysine
- L-Methionine
- Vitamin C
- Iodine
- Zinc
- Manganese
- Chromium
- Selenium
- Chlorophyll
- Sodium alginate
- Apple pectin

These nutrients are best prescribed by a naturopathic doctor.

Chlorophyll

Chlorophyll is the element in plants that makes them green. Chlorophyll chelates heavy metals because it has a porphyrin ring, which binds metal ions.The middle of chlorophyll is magnesium, which is freed under acidic conditions, allowing other heavy metals to bind in its place. Chlorophyll can be taken in drop form. The standard adult dose is five drops a day, mixed in water.

Be careful though, because chlorophyll can stain the teeth. So be sure to dilute it in water. One of my patients was using chlorophyll to freshen her breath and detoxify her metals. She used a few too many drops in her mouth just before an important business meeting and laughed her way to the meeting with her green teeth and tongue. Thank goodness she was a light-hearted person who didn't stress over the ordeal.

Cilantro

Cilantro *(Coriandrum sativum)* is a well-known heavy metal chelator. Cilantro detoxifies mercury, lead and aluminum. Cilantro detoxifies intracellular mercury. It has the added benefit of enhancing digestion as well.

Adult dose: Two capsules twice a day, on empty stomach.

Chlorella

Chlorella is a whole food supplement that helps to detoxify heavy metals and pesticides from the system. It is wonderful because it has the added benefit of improving bowel movements while detoxifying the heavy metals. It also contains vitamins, minerals and enzymes.

Adult dose: Two capsules, twice a day, on empty stomach.

See VitaDetox™ from VitaTree™ Nutritionals at www.vitatree.ca

CHAPTER 6 | CANDIDIASIS AND FUNGAL INFECTIONS

Causes of Candida and Fungus

Candida is a normal organism that lives in the digestive tract and vagina in women. However, it can change to a more invasive, fungal form under certain circumstances. Candidiasis is one of the most common and under-diagnosed conditions that I see in my practice. The medical establishment has downplayed the significance of candida problems, as has the naturopathic community. My belief is that chronic candidiasis is so common that it is only natural that so many doctors are now picking up on it. Systemic fungal disease is becoming more prevalent, because fungus is rampant in our environment.

The main causes of candida include the following:

- Antibiotic use
- Synthetic hormones, steroids
- Diet with too many refined sugars
- Heavy metal toxicity
- Food sensitivities
- Gut dysbiosis
- Hormonal imbalances

Symptoms of Candida

Symptoms of candida overgrowth include, but are not limited to:

- Fatigue
- Yeast infections
- Urinary tract infections
- Athlete's foot, fungal skin infections
- Eczema
- Foggy thinking, headaches, irritability
- Bloating, gas
- Cravings for sugars, carbohydrates
- Inability to lose weight
- Sensitivity to perfumes, soaps, chemicals, tobacco
- Unexplained itchiness of skin

Laboratory Diagnosis of Candida

Candida can be diagnosed in a variety of ways – medically and from a naturopathic perspective. Allopathic doctors usually send a stool sample to the lab to find the number of candida organisms present.

There are other allopathic tests for fungus, such as:

- Sputum samples
- Nail cultures
- Skin biopsies/scrapings

Naturopaths usually evaluate the patient's symptom picture first to determine if candida or fungus is a factor. A naturopath can also employ other tests, such as:

- Biofeedback therapy (Quantum Xrroid SCIO report)
- Live blood microscopy
- Candida questionnaire (see William Crook's The Yeast Connection)
- Sputum samples
- Stool samples

Antibiotics, Synthetic Hormones, Corticosteroids

The overuse of antibiotics is part of the cause of so many chronic candidiasis cases today. Each time you take an antibiotic, the drug wipes out your good and bad gut bacteria. It takes approximately one whole year to regain your normal gut flora after only one round of antibiotics. Fungal organisms can take over the normal flora more easily when the numbers of good bacteria, such as acidophilus and bifidus, are lowered.

Heavy Metal Link

Heavy metal toxicity is linked to fungal infections. Candida is an organism that chelates out heavy metals, mainly mercury and copper. It tries to lessen the load of the heavy metals on the body by partially breaking them down. The broken-down ions of the heavy metal are then more easily excreted by the body. Fungus also depletes the body of essential minerals, which are also needed for heavy metal detoxification. Therefore, the metals are less likely to be metabolized when minerals are deficient, thus making the fungus worse. The vicious cycle continues unless interventions are used to clear up the fungus and heavy metals, and to re-establish the mineral status.

Treat the Cause

Candida and fungus can only survive in the host if the terrain is not healthy. The terrain is the vital energy, immune system and local health of all the internal organs and the blood. If these are all in good working order, fungus and candida in its yeast form have a difficult time surviving. However, stress, poor diet, lack of sleep and exercise can lead to a less healthy terrain, allowing for these organisms to stick around. Therefore, most treatments for fungus and candida include local and systemic remedies. An example of a local treatment would be tea tree oil for athlete's foot. A systemic treatment may be oil of oregano to kill the yeast in the blood. Other adjuncts to the internal antifungal may be immune enhancers and lifestyle changes to lower stress.

Treatments for Chronic Candidiasis

Treatments for candidiasis vary from one practitioner to another. I have found the best combination to be the following because it is easy to follow and patient compliance is the greatest.

- Treat underlying cause of candida overgrowth, that is, hormonal imbalance, heavy metal toxicity, antibiotic use
- Immune system regulation and modulation, using herbal and homeopathic immune enhancers
- Detoxification remedies, homeopathic drainage remedies for the liver, kidneys, lungs, lymph, skin and digestive tract
- Oregano oil in emulsified tablet form that kills candida quickly, as well as other parasites and bacteria

Oregano oil has two phenolic compounds: Thymol and carvacrol, which have antioxidant properties. Emulsified oregano oil is preferred over liquid forms, as emulsification means that the oil is broken down into smaller molecules for increased surface area, better absorption and less burden to the liver. The sustained release allows the oil to spend more time in the digestive tract where it kills offending organisms

i. Beginning adult dose: Two tablets, two times a day, after meals
ii. Contraindicated for pregnant or breastfeeding mothers.

- Probiotics using human-derived microflora
  i. Dose: One capsule three times a day, with meals

- Modified candida diet: Limited sugar, alcohol, yeast and carbohydrates
  i. Two fruits a day, maximum
  ii. One treat a day with refined sugar (e.g., one cookie)
  iii. Two alcoholic drinks a week
  iv. Avoid bread and wheat products made with yeast

- Dietary fibre, which increases elimination of offending candida organisms
  i. Beginning adult dose: Start with 1/8 teaspoon psyllium husks at bedtime with a full 8 oz. glass of water
  ii. Increase vegetable consumption

- Grapefruit seed extract kills candida; used for maintenance or if oregano is not well tolerated
  i. Adult dose: Five drops mixed well in water or small amount of juice to mask the taste, taken three times daily, just after a meal
  ii. Tastes horrible and is quite thick, so it needs to be well stirred
  iii. Must always be diluted, never taken alone
  iv. Available in tablets for those who can't stand the taste

- Certain minerals are depleted by fungus and need to be replaced. These include selenium, taurine, iron, manganese and magnesium. (Caution: Aggravations are possible when minerals are re-introduced because the fungus is first fed by the minerals before it is eradicated)

Note: The above suggestions are only given for reference. Medical consultation with a naturopathic doctor is recommended to avoid side effects.

Diet

Some practitioners will recommend a very strict anti-candida diet, which eliminates all sugar (even fruits), alcohol, yeasts, fermented foods, wheat and dairy. I find most patients find it very difficult to stick to such a regimented diet. However, there is the odd person who likes this type of restrictive regime. Most patients find it easier to simply cut down the yeast-forming foods and take the supplements as suggested. The reason that sugar is eliminated is because candida multiplies when fed carbohydrates and sugars. It also multiplies if foods are undigested or partially digested. Typically, foods to which you are sensitive are not properly broken down in the digestive process. These foods also feed the candida.

Healing Crisis

It is quite possible to have an aggravation when killing off the fungus in the body. Fungal molecules are like little bags full of stuff. The stuff inside is many protein molecules. When you start to kill the fungus, these bags open up and the proteins spill out into the surrounding tissue. The proteins are also fungal organisms. It is quite common to have more fungal symptoms when you first start to kill them. For example, if your fungus was in the form of athlete's foot, your feet may become itchier and ooze more fluid when you begin a candida cleanse. It is very important to stay on the supplements that kill the fungus during the aggravation to ensure that all of these protein particles of fungus are eradicated.

Free Radicals

A free radical is defined as an atom or group of atoms that is highly chemically reactive because it has at least one unpaired electron. Free radicals are unstable molecules that run through the body, looking for free electrons to make them more stable. In stealing electrons, free radicals cause other cells to become free radicals and unstable. A domino effect occurs and thus, disrupts cell function.

Free radical damage is caused by the following:

- A normal part of metabolism
- After exercise
- Exposure to sunlight
- Environmental toxins
- Heavy metal toxins
- Exposure to electromagnetic pollution (cell phone, microwaves)
- Cigarette smoke

Free radical damage to cells is believed to be a causative factor for the aging process and ailments such as heart disease and cancer.

What saves us from free radicals?

Antioxidants are stable molecules that have the ability to donate electrons to free radicals without becoming free radicals themselves. The most popular antioxidants are vitamins C, E, A, and selenium. Recent studies have shown that antioxidants in fruits and vegetables may have a more positive effect on free radicals because they contain not only the above-mentioned vitamins and minerals, but also thousands of phytonutrients, that work synergistically to combat the damage. The longer I have practised as a naturopathic doctor, the more I have shied away from prescribing synthetic vitamins and minerals. The synthetic formulation of these nutrients lacks the important co-factors and phytonutrients found naturally in foods. For this reason, I recommend that patients increase their antioxidant status by taking whole food antioxidants in supplement form.

Some of the well-studied phytochemical antioxidants found in foods includes carotenoids, flavonoids, isothiocyanates and phenols.

Carotenoids

Brightly coloured fruits and vegetables (carrots, red peppers, sweet potatoes, tomatoes) are rich in carotenoids. Different carotenoids may be more beneficial than others, such as:

- Xanthophylls, including lutein and zeaxanthin, are found in the lenses of the eye and have proven effective in the prevention of cataract formation in the eyes. Xanthophylls can be obtained from dark green, leafy vegetables, such as spinach, broccoli and eggs.
- Lycopene is an important carotenoid that may also play an important role in eye health as a person ages. Tomatoes are a good source of lycopene.
- Beta carotene is the most widely studied carotenoid and is a powerful antioxidant.

Flavonoids

Flavonoids are compounds that are commonly found in nature and are classified in groups: Flavonols, flavones, flavanones, isoflavones, catechins, anthocyanidins and chalcones. Over 4,000 flavonoids have been identified, and they are usually found in fruits and vegetables. The flavonoids have been vastly studied because of their potentially beneficial effects on human health – they are reported to have antiviral, anti-allergic, anti-platelet, anti-inflammatory, anti-tumour and antioxidant properties.[33] Some important characteristics and sources of flavonoids are listed below:

- Flavanones are found in citrus fruits and neutralize free radicals and prevent cellular degeneration

- Flavanols are found in green tea, apples and grapes. They maintain heart health and circulation

- Anthocyanidins are found in berries, cherries and grapes. They maintain brain function and increase cellular antioxidant function

- Proanthocyanidins can be found in cranberries, cocoa, apples, grapes and wine, and maintain a healthy urinary tract

Isothiocyanates

These powerful antioxidants are to be found in cruciferous vegetables, and have anti-tumour effects, such as sulforaphane, which is found in cauliflower, broccoli, kale and cabbage.

Phenols

These include caffeic and ferulic acids, and are found in apples, pears, and citrus fruits. They maintain heart health and vision.

The ORAC Scale

Oxygen Radical Absorbance Capacity (ORAC) is a method of measuring antioxidant capacities of different foods. It was developed at the National Institute of Aging in Baltimore, Maryland. The following is a list of fruits and vegetables with the highest ORAC values:

Fruits – Goji berries, acai berries, prunes, raisins, blueberries, cranberries, pomegranates, acerola cherries, apples, pineapples, grapes and papaya

Vegetables – Kale, garlic, spinach, Brussels sprouts, broccoli, beets, red peppers, tomatoes, carrots and green tea

Based on extensive research on the healing properties of fruits and vegetables, I formulated a supplement containing all of the above ingredients. For more information, visit www.vitatree.ca

CHAPTER 7 | NATUROPATHIC REMEDIES FOR DETOXIFYING THE BODY

Listen to Your Body

Your body tells you exactly when it is out of balance. A headache, sore throat or rash are all examples of symptoms that your body manifests as a wake-up call. These are "red flags" that signal something is wrong and needs to be fixed. Unfortunately, millionaires, or aspiring ones, are so caught up in their daily lives that they ignore symptoms until they get so bad that they are debilitating. I don't know how many times I have come down with a cold and "pressed on" – working as much as usual without taking a break. I usually end up being sick for weeks with a low-grade infection when I don't take the time I need to get well. If I would just take a day or two in bed, I would be well in a few days rather than weeks. I know – I'm not the only one.

Thankfully, my example of a cold is not life-threatening. However, those who ignore chronic complaints can end up being very sick with serious conditions in the long run. People think that diseases such as cancer just pop up one day. In fact, most cancers take years and years to grow. There are almost always signs of toxicity before a tumour develops, based on the laws of homotoxicology. The more the toxins build up, without an outlet for excretion, the deeper the toxins penetrate in the system, eventually causing tumours and growths. The good news is that this can all be prevented with detoxification. I strongly recommend the guidance and advice of a naturopathic doctor who is trained at recognizing signs and symptoms of toxicity. You may think a symptom you have is not important, however, to a naturopath it may be a very clear indication of underlying toxicity that needs to be cleared.

Sleep

Proper sleep is the most overlooked, but simple, detoxification necessity. Those who are aspiring or accomplished millionaires often know this subject very well. Long work hours, or nights spent awake due to excitement or anticipation, often affect this group of individuals more than others. During sleep, the body repairs itself and the immune system is most active at this time. Melatonin, the hormone secreted during sleep, helps to stimulate the immune system. It helps to stimulate the secretion of thymosin, a hormone secreted by the thymus gland, one of the centres of the immune system.[34] Melatonin also increases the action of natural killer cells, which help to ward off cancer cells.

During sleep, the liver is most active, working to detoxify most of the chemicals that are circulated throughout the body. Those who lack proper sleep do not get the full benefits of detoxification through the liver that occurs naturally.

Everyone needs a different amount of sleep at night. So, I always ask my patients how many hours a night their body needs for sleep, and then how many are they presently sleeping? Most patients do not get their required amount of sleep, and, therefore, their bodies show it. The most common complaints of those who don't get enough sleep are, of course, fatigue, and poor immunity to infections, colds and flus. I usually tell these people that I can give them every remedy I have for their immune system and their energy, but if they don't get enough sleep, they will likely not get much better.

Lack of sleep also affects one's emotional status. If you look at children whose nap time has been delayed, this is usually when they are most irritable and difficult to deal with. The same is true for adults – only we pay less attention to our need for sleep. This is why we can be just as cranky as our children.

Multivitamins and Minerals

It is very difficult to get all the nutrients we need from food. Our soils have been depleted from over-farming for years. The amount of pollution we face daily increases our bodies' needs for nutrients. This means we would need to consume four to five times the amount of food as usual, in order to get all the nutrients required in a day.

Supplementation is very specific for each individual. However, there are still some standard supplements that I believe most people should be taking. I usually suggest a good-quality multivitamin/mineral supplement for my patients. I recommend whole food vitamins. Most vitamins found today in pharmacies and health food stores are not whole food supplements. They are generally synthetic forms of the vitamins and minerals that are extracted using various chemicals, and often lack the important co-factors and accessory nutrients required for the proper absorption and digestion of the vitamins and minerals.

Vitamin C is a good example of a nutrient that is synthetically made in most supplements. Usually corn (which may be genetically modified) is used as the source from which vitamin C is made. The corn is treated with enzymes, acetone, sulphuric acid, sodium hydroxide and alcohol to derive ascorbic acid (vitamin C). How can the use of so many chemicals to form an essential nutrient be healthy? In nature, vitamin C never occurs in isolation as one component such as ascorbic acid. Vitamin C actually has six components, ascorbic acid being one of them. All six components of vitamin C work together, to provide the beneficial effects of the nutrient. By taking just ascorbic acid, you run the risk of depleting other nutrients and co-factors necessary to help the ascorbic acid function optimally.

When we eat food, the nutrient composition of the food is in the perfect balance for those nutrients to be best absorbed. Synthetic vitamins lose this important quality in their processing. The next best thing to good-quality food is a vitamin made from the foods that are whole and unprocessed. Some vitamin manufacturers have developed a way to grow organic plants to be high in vitamins, minerals, enzymes, fibre, trace elements, essential fatty acids, DNA and RNA. These unique vitamins are called "whole food vitamins and minerals." Whole food means that the whole plant is used, not just the isolated nutrient that has been chemically denatured – the way most vitamin supplements are. These vitamins are a step above synthetic nutrients, yet not as beneficial as 100 per cent whole food vitamins. Whole food extracts, usually freeze-dried, maintain most – if not all – the important phytonutrients from the whole food source.

Labels on supplements can be confusing and somewhat misleading. "Natural" means it has the element carbon in it. "Natural source" means it is derived from a plant. Synthetic nutrients can be called natural when really they are not. The term to look for is "100% whole food."

Testing Supplement Compatibility

Supplement compatibility with a patient can be tested using various methods. I often test my patients with their indicated supplements, to be sure that they will have a positive reaction. For instance, if I have two types of multivitamins, I will test both to see which one reacts best. I either use a small machine that tests the electromagnetism of an individual when a supplement is introduced, or I do applied kinesiology (AK), which is more commonly known as muscle testing. The patient holds the supplement in their hand and I test their arm strength to see if their muscle locks or not. By comparing the muscle strength with its baseline strength (from earlier testing without the supplement), I can determine whether or not the supplement is helpful or not. The advantage of testing compatibility is the ability to fine-tune supplementation for each individual.

Green Supplements

It is my belief that a good-quality green supplement is essential for most people – especially those who do not eat enough vegetables daily. Green supplements are loaded with essential nutrients, such as chlorophyll, minerals and trace minerals. Some people experience a slight detoxification reaction when beginning a green supplement, so I encourage them to start with an amount smaller than is stated on the package, and then increase gradually from there. Green supplements are generally taken once a day, on an empty stomach, mixed in water or a little juice mixed with water. Vegetable capsules are also a good way to supplement green foods in a whole food format. See my formulation VitaVeggies™ at www.vitatree.ca

Antioxidants

Antioxidant means "against oxidation." When a cell uses oxygen, toxic by-products or free radicals are formed. Free radicals attach to stable molecules and take an electron in the process. When the once stable molecule loses its electron, it becomes a free radical. This domino effect results in continuous damage in the body, leading to disease and aging. Antioxidants stabilize free radicals by donating one of their electrons. However, the antioxidant can itself become a free radical after it has given up its electron.

Detoxification Supplements

There are many different types of detoxification supplements available today. They range from herbal preparations and teas, to homeopathic complexes and detoxification packages. I always caution people about the possible negative side effects of these regimens. Some are also much too strong. Everyone is in a different state of toxicity, which changes within his or her own lifetime. For example, a woman who has just had a baby is somewhat less toxic than before her pregnancy, because the baby detoxified many of her toxins. Others may be more toxic after recent exposure to fumes and chemicals, for instance, after painting the house. For this reason, it is imperative to seek the advice of a naturopath to determine what type of detoxification would be most beneficial, and what strength of remedies would do the job – without causing too much of an aggravation or a *healing crisis.*

A healing crisis is the body's abrupt reaction to detoxification. Generally, a healing crisis feels a lot like a cold or flu usually, with some form of discharge from the body. It is the body's way of releasing many toxins at once – or over a period of a few days. A healing crisis can occur at any time during a detoxification process and is usually an annoyance, but not harmful.

CASE study

Janet, a forty-three-year-old executive, had the chief complaint of chronic sinus infections. She had suffered with this condition for over twenty years. After a thorough intake and physical exam, I prescribed a series of homeopathic remedies to drain her sinuses and modulate her immune function. She called me in a panic when she had flu-like symptoms and couldn't stop blowing her nose. I explained that it was quite possibly a detoxification reaction and her body was expelling the accumulated toxins. She felt more at ease after my explanation and felt better in a day. From that time on, she experienced no further sinus infections and her breathing was clear.

Weight Loss Supplements

Many are always looking for the "magic pill" or formula for weight loss. Unfortunately, it doesn't exist. There are, however, some supplements that help to shed excess pounds more quickly, when used in conjunction with healthy eating and exercise. I will mention a few that I have found effective, even though I'm sure many more are available and work very well. The reason I have chosen the following is that they do not contain caffeine, ephedra or other stimulants, which can have a long-term negative effects on overall health.

Protein powders

There are a variety of protein powders on the market today. Most are either whey-based or from soy. I tend to recommend the soy formulas more often than whey because most people digest soy better than dairy-based formulas. Protein is essential in the production of lean muscle mass. Protein deficiency and carbohydrate overload can lead to obesity.

Soy protein is a well-rounded, plant-based protein source that is easily digested.

Green tea

Green tea has been found to be helpful in fat loss while exercising. It appears that the caffeine content, as well as specific compounds called catechin polyphenols, has an effect on fat oxidation and the activation of thermogenesis for weight loss.[35]

Green tea is included in many weight loss supplements in the form of green tea extract. I usually suggest drinking two cups of organic green tea per day, between meals

Supplement Absorption

SUPPLEMENT	WITH FOOD	EMPTY STOMACH
Herbs		Better absorption on empty stomach, 1/2 hour before food or 2 - 3 hours after a meal
Vitamins	Better with food, because digestive enzymes secreted while eating help to break down the vitamin	
Minerals (e.g., calcium, magnesium)	Better with food, as with vitamins	Calcium can be taken just before bed
Digestive enzymes	For improving digestion take at beginning of a meal	To reduce inflammation, take 1/2 hour before a meal or 2 - 3 hours after a meal
Probiotics (acidophilus, bifidus)	See manufacturer's guidelines. Human microflora is better with food	Soil organisms are generally better on an empty stomach
Homeopathic remedies		Between meals without any strong flavours in the mouth, such as toothpaste, coffee or chewing gum

Vitamin B3 is niacin and can cause a "niacin flush" in some people, even at a low dose. An itchy, red rash appears soon after taking niacin, and disappears in minutes to hours. The rash is not harmful, but may be too irritating for some people. Niacinamide or non-flush niacin is available as an alternative to niacin for vitamin B3.

Supplement dosage

Dosages vary for each individual, again depending on the toxicity load. The dosages listed on the bottle are not necessarily accurate. Canadian and American labelling laws require that the manufacturer give directions for use on the bottle. Nevertheless, the best advice is always from your naturopathic doctor. This is especially true for single dose homeopathic remedies. They often say to take three or four pellets, three times daily, which is hardly ever recommended by a homeopath or naturopath. Homeopathic remedies are usually sugar pellets made from lactose that have the remedy coated on the outside of the pellet. The standard way to take the pellets is to let them dissolve under your tongue. For alternative ways to dose homeopathic remedies, the naturopath may suggest that you put the pellet in water and then take a sip of the water as one dose. For babies, you can wet your finger, touch the pellet and then put your finger in the baby's mouth for one dose.

Dosing for herbal remedies varies according to the weight of the person taking the herb. To determine the dose for children aged two and older, follow the rule:

$$\frac{\textbf{Weight of child in kilograms x adult dose}}{70}$$

or

$$\frac{\textbf{Weight of child in pounds x adult dose}}{150}$$

Infants under twelve months that are breastfed can get the exact dose needed, if the mother takes the adult dosage of the herb.

Dietary Changes

Before I suggest any dietary changes for a patient, I usually ask him or her to fill out a diet diary for seven days (like the example below). You can photocopy this diet diary and use it yourself.

	MON	TUES	WED	THURS	FRI	SAT	SUN
BREAKFAST							
LUNCH							
DINNER							
SYMPTOMS / ENERGY							

It is important to write down serving sizes and all fluid intake for the week. The last row of the diet diary leaves space where you can fill in how you are feeling on each day. This is helpful in relating what you are eating to your symptoms.

I find the diet diary is a great exercise in becoming conscious of what you are eating. So many of us stuff food into our mouths without even thinking about it. Conscious eating means appreciating food for its nourishment and ability to keep us healthy. Many are surprised when they see on paper how much they eat in a day.

A common mistake that I have observed on diet diaries is that people tend to eat the same foods over and over again. Whether it's out of habit, neglect or ignorance, eating the same thing day after day is not healthy for the system. Foods that are repeated too often become toxic to the digestive tract. Most people who follow their intuition when it comes to eating will realize that their system can only tolerate the same food for so long.

Also, food sensitivities can easily develop when the same food is repeated frequently in the diet. Once you become sensitive to a food, you may have to avoid it altogether for a few months to desensitize your system.

Fasting/Juicing

The definition of fasting is a total or partial abstinence from food or water for a period of time. For centuries, fasting has been practised for religious and physiological reasons, as well as due to illness. Famous fasters include Hippocrates, Plato and Socrates. The physiological benefits of fasting have been studied. What was discovered was there is little vitamin or mineral loss, skin diseases improved, blood pressure decreased, triglycerides and cholesterol decreased, cataracts decreased, while immunity increased.

Fasting should always be done under medical supervision as ketosis [the breakdown of fat cells for the production of energy] can develop and may be dangerous for some people. It is usually recommended that a fast be done in warmer weather when the body naturally needs less food. People who should not fast include children, pregnant and lactating women, and those with poor kidney function.

Juicing is one way of fasting that is relatively safe and effective for a short-term detoxification process. There are varying degrees of quality in juicers on the market. If you do not own a juicer, the next best thing is to use a common blender to blend the fruits and vegetables in water and strain the denser particles. If you purchase juice, it should be freshly made (within the last ten minutes), because after that the nutrients oxidize and have little benefit.

I usually suggest that people work their way up to a juice fast. Below is a common prescription of mine.

Janine's Juice Fast

Juices need to be freshly prepared and consumed within ten minutes of preparation – after that, nutrients and enzymes are lost. Vegetable juices are preferable to fruit juices because they have a lower glycemic index, are easier on the pancreas and aid in faster weight loss. Use lots of dark green, leafy veggies and add carrots for taste. Beets are especially good for the kidneys and aid as a diuretic.

Day 1:	Eat fresh fruits and vegetables, lean protein (chicken, fish), whole grains (e.g., brown rice, millet, quinoa), 2 (8 oz.) glasses of freshly pressed vegetable or fruit juice
Day 2:	Same as above, but eliminate grains, 3 (8 oz.) glasses of juice
Day 3:	Same as Day 2, no protein or grains, fresh fruits and vegetables are allowed, 3 (8 oz.) glasses of juice
Day 4:	Only 4 – 5 (8 oz.) glasses of juice, mostly vegetable
Day 5:	Same as Day 3
Day 6:	Same as Day 2
Day 7:	Same as Day 1

Water should be consumed throughout each day. Herbal teas are also permitted – without milk, sweetener or caffeine. Light exercise, such as stretching or yoga, is advised during a fast, as well as fifteen to twenty minutes of sunshine each day. Plenty of rest is also helpful.

The juices chosen should be ones to which you have no known sensitivity. The advantage of working in this step-wise manner is that you ease your body into the fast. The toxic load is then released more slowly and the likelihood of an aggravation from the fast is minimized. Some aggravation symptoms are as follows: Headache, nausea, drowsiness, foggy thinking, light-headedness and fatigue. Contraindications to fasting include being underweight, diabetes, pregnancy, prescription drugs and eating disorders.

Chinese Remedies for Detoxification

Chinese medicine, both herbal and dietary, can be very helpful for detoxification and improving the function of the internal organs. The Chinese believe that the diet is very much related to the seasons, and the different tastes of food have different healing abilities. The foundation of health comes from the ability to transform food into energy for the body. The Chinese always try to balance yin and yang, which are two types of energy in the body. Yin is cold and fluid, whereas yang is hot and more solid. If there is an imbalance between yin and yang, illness can arise. Foods all have different properties from a Chinese perspective and can be hot, cold, warm, cool or neutral. These classifications do not refer to the actual temperature of the food, but the effects they have when eaten. So, for instance, if someone is very yang and they have too much heat in their system, they will improve by eating more cooling foods.

In general, it is advisable to consume warming foods in the winter, when our bodies tend to be cooler. This helps to balance yin and yang, cold and hot. The opposite is true in the summer, when we tend to be warmer; it is best to eat cooling foods. For example, eat more salads in the summer (cooling), and soups in the winter (warming). If you pay attention to your intuition, you probably do this already anyway.

CASE study

The wife of a successful multimillionaire was concerned about their daughter, age five, who had suffered from eczema for years. Her skin was red and scaly and she noticed that whenever she became too hot, her itching got worse. Her tongue was very red and her pulse fast. (The Chinese diagnose illness by looking at the tongue and feeling the pulse in three positions on each wrist). She was too yang. I suggested that she avoid hot foods (see chart), and concentrate on eating as many cold or cool foods as possible. After two weeks, she was feeling much better and her skin was improving dramatically. Her mother even noticed that if she ate one of the hot foods, she became more irritated again.

HOT	WARM	NEUTRAL	COOL	COLD
Ginger Cayenne Pepper Garlic Onions Chives Cinnamon Ginseng Lamb Goat Moose Deer	Chicken Carrot Peanut Orange	Grape Rice Plum Strawberry Beef Chamomile tea	Barley Green lentil Lemon Raw tomato	Green apple Banana Celery Cucumber Lettuce Melon Pear Asparagus Yogurt Squash Fish Shrimp Lobster Crab

In Chinese medicine, the different flavours of foods affect the internal organs in either a positive or negative way. The following chart depicts suggestions of foods that may be helpful or harmful for the organs listed.

THE FIVE FLAVOURS OF FOODS

FLAVOUR	SWEET	SOUR	PUNGENT	SALTY	BITTER
Examples:	Root vegetables (carrots, sweet potatoes, beets, squash), Pumpkin, Beef	Lemons, Olives, Tomatoes, Apples, Citrus fruits, Blueberries, Cranberries, Raspberries	Mint, Basil, Garlic, Onion, Ginger, Curry, Fennel, Chives, Radish, Lamb Wine Alcohol	Seafood (shrimp, lobster, crab), Seaweed, Salt, Pork	Parsley, Artichoke, Brussels sprouts, Cabbage, Broccoli, Rapini, Coffee, Chocolate
Good for:	Digestion in spleen and stomach	Liver, Gallbladder	Lungs, Large intestine	Kidneys, Bladder	Heart, Small intestine
Bad for:	Kidneys, Bladder	Digestion in spleen and stomach	Liver, Gallbladder	Heart, Small intestine	Lungs, Large intestine

Based on the information in this chart, there are some interesting explanations as to why some foods aggravate certain conditions. For instance, citrus fruit juices are not helpful for digestion. If you have a weak stomach and spleen, according to Chinese medicine, too much orange juice would produce high acidity levels in the stomach, perhaps leading to an ulcer. Even though orange juice is rich in vitamins, they would not be absorbed, if the acidity level was too high.

Salty foods are not helpful for the heart, if the heart is weak. In the wintertime, the heart is an organ system that has lower energy compared with the warmer months, in Chinese medicine. For this reason, eating salty foods in the winter is not as healthy as in the summer – when you perspire more and need more salt to replace electrolytes lost in perspiration.

Good news for coffee drinkers and chocolate lovers: Bitter foods, such as chocolate and coffee, are generally helpful in the winter months (when we crave them more), because they strengthen the heart that tends to be weak.[36]

Acupuncture

Acupuncture is also an effective way to detoxify the major organs. Energy or chi that flows through the acupuncture meridians on the body can become stuck or stagnant. By inserting needles into the acupuncture points, the chi can be stimulated and allowed to flow more freely. This has a detoxification effect on the internal organ to which the acupuncture point is connected.

Hydrotherapy

Hydrotherapy is the use of water for healing. A standard practice for hydrotherapy is to alternate between hot and cold water in the shower. This can include the use of a sauna and then jumping into a cold shower. This fluctuation between hot and cold causes a pumping action in the blood that can be very effective at clearing toxins. The hot water causes a dilation of the blood vessels, and the cold water causes the vessels to constrict. For an alternating hot and cold shower, you should start with hot water for about three minutes, then change to cold for as long as you can stand, then back to hot again, and so on for a total of three hot and three cold, always ending with cold. This is a wonderful way to stimulate the immune system, the nervous system and digestion. Spas around the world offer hydrotherapy baths, usually a hot bath situated close to a cold one. Based on the same premise, it is suggested that you soak in the hot bath first and then jump in the cold one and vice versa, always ending in cold. This type of therapy is contraindicated for people with severe circulation problems, heart abnormalities and those who cannot tolerate the cold.

Colonics, or colon therapy, is the use of water and other nutrients in the rectum and large intestine for cleansing purposes. A solution of water and occasionally herbs, oxygen, probiotics and other healing ingredients are released into the colon by the therapist. As the water is released from the colon after the procedure, fecal material trapped in the pockets and folds of the colon is dislodged. This cleanses the entire five feet of colon, unlike an enema that only flushes the eight to twelve inches of the sigmoid colon. Once all this debris has been removed, the stage has been set in the colon for the growth of healthy micro-organisms.

Colonics are certainly not for everyone. The patients I have seen that have had colonics have found them very helpful. I have also heard of a few not-so-pleasant results where patients have had a lot of gas and distension after a colonic. As with any therapy, you have to be comfortable with the procedure and possible side effects. Colonics are not recommended in pregnancy, appendicitis, severe heart disease, severe hemorrhoids, diverticulosis or diverticulitis, obstruction, cancer and any bleeding in the GI tract due to severe inflammatory bowel disease.

CASE study

(Warning: DO NOT READ if you have a weak stomach). Denise, a woman in her late thirties, came into my office complaining of lethargy, depression, fibromyalgia-like pains, headaches, abdominal discomfort, digestive complaints and being overweight. She had recently been for a colonic, but very little was voided during the procedure. It was suggested that she try Metamucil. She had a few foul-smelling bowel movements and was curious, so she put on some rubber gloves and inspected the odd-looking stool. She noticed a long, thick object – a tapeworm, which was over one-foot long. She didn't see the head of the worm, which meant she had to do further treatment to "purge the beast."

Homeopathic Drainage

Homeopathic drainage is a homeopathic prescribing technique used to assist the detoxification of major organs by using low-potency homeopathics. The idea of drainage using homeopathy originated in Europe, when homeopathic doctors started to realize that constitutional remedies did not work as well as they once did. They concluded that the increasing amounts of environmental toxins were causing their own effects and symptoms for the patients – sometimes masking their true homeopathic state. It became more in vogue for homeopathic practitioners to use drainage remedies first, and then re-evaluate the patient's case for a constitutional homeopathic remedy.

Practitioners who use drainage remedies usually categorize their patients in one or more of the reaction modes of disease. Reaction modes are a measure of a person's vitality that helps to gauge how they should be treated, what remedies may be required, and how well they will tolerate the treatment. The four main reaction modes are as follows, with their typical corresponding symptom pictures and characteristics:

Psoric

Energetic, reactive, high-strung individuals who usually excrete toxins right away. When these people get sick, they get very sick all at once and get better very quickly. They usually have a fever (a good sign in naturopathic medicine as it kills bacteria and viruses). Children are usually in this reaction mode, especially if they are not vaccinated. (This is the healthiest reaction mode).

Sycotic

Calm, indifferent, tired, individuals. These patients eliminate most toxins, but some remain in the body. When they get sick, they usually are not as violently ill, and their recovery time is a bit longer than the psoric type.

Tuberculinic

Fatigued individuals that become drained from any illness or emotional challenge. Their systems tend to continue to accumulate toxins with very few being excreted.

Luetic

These individuals have lost all energy to fight off and excrete toxins. They develop degenerative diseases and form tumours. Their bodies become even more imbalanced when they react to toxins.

The use of combination remedies would hope to move the person up the ladder towards the psoric reaction mode, or miasm. Homeopathic remedies are capable of reversing disease processes – even the most deleterious, such as cancer (which is a luetic reaction mode).

Yoga

Yoga, in my opinion, is one of the best forms of exercise because it helps to detoxify at a physical, mental/emotional and spiritual level. As mentioned in Chapter Three, there are specific yoga postures to speed up elimination in the major detoxification organs. Yoga can be practised by anyone, at any age, and at any level. Yoga is an exercise that is not only a current trend in exercise circles, but an ancient method of clearing the system of unwanted accumulations.

Yoga postures allow blood to pool in organs, which stimulates those organs to function more efficiently. After the posture is released, blood rushes out of the organ, removing toxins. For example, if you perform the side angle stretch to the right side, blood pools in the liver. When you release out of the posture, blood rushes out of the area and then to the spleen when you perform the posture on the left side as you would traditionally do.

One of my past yoga instructors told me about a detoxification reaction she had from an intense yoga training retreat. She said that after two days of doing at least eight hours of yoga a day, her face broke out with a severe red rash that lasted for about a week. She explained that the postures and intense focus on the breath for such an extended period of time helped to push the toxins to the surface of the skin.

CASE study

Linda, a thirty-three-year-old woman who was also a patient of mine, said that after each yoga class that she did, she would become jaundiced or yellow. This was due to her liver dumping large amounts of toxins and bilirubin into the bloodstream to be processed. Linda was active in many other sports, but only the yoga caused this reaction.

Contraindications for Detoxification Protocols

Pregnancy and Lactation

Pregnancy is a delicate time in a woman's life. The growing baby is a woman's best detoxifier. The baby has fresh organs of detoxification – a brand-new liver, lungs, skin, kidneys and digestive tract. Even though these organs in the baby are still immature, they begin to detoxify early in their development. It is for this reason that women need to be especially careful that they do not expose themselves to toxic chemicals during pregnancy. Some detoxification, such as homeopathic drainage, is safe in pregnancy, but only under the advice of a naturopathic doctor. A simple and generally safe detoxification that helps with nausea in pregnancy is to use fresh lemon juice in water and drink throughout the day. Nausea in pregnancy is often associated with hormonal changes, but also liver toxicity. The more toxic a woman is before she becomes pregnant, the higher the likelihood of nausea. I generally recommend that both the man and woman detoxify prior to conception, to diminish the effects of toxicity on the mom and baby.

Lactation also is a relative contraindication for detoxification. However, if a baby is experiencing symptoms due to toxicity, such as eczema, it may be helpful for the mother to take detoxification remedies that pass through the breast milk to the baby. Again, these protocols should only be prescribed by a naturopathic doctor, and are specific to the baby and mother in each case.

Depleted vitality and/or severe chronic illness

In the case of serious chronic disease, it is often more important to increase the stamina, immunity and energy of the individual before commencing a detoxification protocol. Detoxification can aggravate someone who is severely ill, and may not even occur effectively if the patient does not have the energy to complete the detoxification processes. The first recommendations would be to increase nutritional support and immune status before attempting any detoxification in such a case.

CHAPTER 8 | DETOXIFICATION OF THE MIND

The Mind/Body Connection, Stress and Affluence

Scientists have been trying to prove for years that the mind has an effect on the physical processes of the body. There are now numerous studies that prove the connection. One of the pioneers in this field of work is Dr. Candace Pert, a researcher in the field of psychoneuroimmunoendocrinology. She and others have proven that the mind has a biochemical effect on the physiology of our bodies. In other words, what we think and feel emotionally is reflected in the way our bodies function on a physical level. In Dr. Pert's book *Molecules of Emotion*, she relates how she found the mind is definitely connected to the body. She was able to identify peptides that were secreted during certain emotions. These peptides had a predictable physiological effect on target tissues. This proved that molecules of emotion existed, and could be quantitatively evaluated.

A good example of this is when some people run to the washroom when they are stressed out. The peptides in the brain signalled by stress travel to the intestines to signal bowel movements. If the mind has this much power to make you leave your present location to run and find a bathroom, could it not have the same power to cause ailments? The answer is: Yes. Stress-induced negative thoughts can eventually ruin your health. They cause negative energy to fester and change the normal functioning of cells. Fortunately, on the other side of the coin, positive thoughts can heal the body.

So if emotions directly affect our physical body, doesn't it make sense to be in control of our thoughts so as to not allow negative ones to take over? So the million-dollar question is this: How do you prevent or stop the negative, fearful emotions from influencing you? There are a few ways that I suggest to my patients on how to clear these thoughts, as seen in the chart on the next page.

TECHNIQUE TO ELIMINATE NEGATIVE THOUGHTS	METHOD
The elastic band technique	Wear a comfortably fitted rubber band (not cutting off circulation) on your wrist. Every time you have a negative thought, snap the band on your wrist. This is a way to snap yourself out of your pattern of negative thoughts.
Meditation	Find a quiet, comfortable place to close your eyes and take a few deep breaths. Know that your problems are only a means to make you learn to be a better person.
Visualization	Go to your happy place. Visualize a place in which you are most happy. It could be at a beach, a waterfall, or the top of a mountain. Close your eyes and visualize yourself there. Smell the air, hear the surroundings, and picture yourself in total bliss. Your brain doesn't know the difference between actually physically being there and just visualizing it. Soon your body will react via chemical messengers to make you feel as if you are there, and problems seem to melt away.

So how does this all relate to acquiring and maintaining affluence? Affluence has difficulty entering a life of negative thoughts, fears and stress. If you are looking to acquire affluence, believe me, it comes much more easily and gracefully when you are relaxed, motivated and pleased with your life. When you are doubtful, negative and stressed, there is a block in energy entering your life. That block of energy stops affluence in its tracks. What the Universe had in store for you may be thwarted because you were too negative to receive it. To allow the Universe to direct affluence your way, the channel to receive it must be open.

Self-Esteem

Our minds can control how we feel mentally, physically and spiritually. The old cliché, "the mind is a powerful thing," is a great understatement. Our thoughts determine our success or failure in anything we do. The basis for a healthy outlook on life is to have positive self-esteem.

It is especially important for an entrepreneur to have positive self-esteem. Often, entrepreneurs have to take risks that most others choose not to. In order to take these risks, an entrepreneur has to feel some level of positive self-worth in order to put him or herself out there. Presenting new ideas, projects or products takes guts! Without a positive sense of self, these presentations can be less than fruitful. I believe many would-be entrepreneurs don't make it simply based on the fact that their self-esteem is not substantial enough. Believe me, it is easy to spot someone with low self-esteem when you have a little yourself.

Part of taking care of our health involves taking care of the way we feel about ourselves. So many of us have had or continue to have a negative self-image. If we don't have a good relationship with ourselves, how are we supposed to have good relationships with anyone else? Loving yourself is the best thing you can do for your health. The body responds positively to positive energy. If you constantly bathe yourself in self-love, little can go wrong. So then why do so many of us beat ourselves up? We have been programmed to believe that we are not good enough by society, our parents, friends and acquaintances. However, when we have the love for ourselves within, the opinions of others do not matter. We know that we are perfect in God's eyes, so do any other eyes matter?

I recently asked a patient, "How is your self-esteem?" She answered, "Oh, I think I look pretty good." I think this would be the response of many, thinking that self-esteem only has to do with the way we look. However, self-worth and esteem are so much more. Our sense of self encompasses the body, mind and spirit and how they relate to each other. Sure, we may be happy about our outside appearance, and that surely is a part of positive thinking towards ourselves. Feeling good about our mental and spiritual health also goes a long way towards positive self-esteem.

CASE study

Evan, a successful fifty-year old man, was having difficulty in his practice as a lawyer. He never worried financially about his life, because business was always steady. He started to be less busy over the course of a few weeks, which then turned into months. His self-esteem plummeted. The more negative he was towards himself, I said, the less business he would attract because the negative energy that surrounded him would only repel people. Evan began to meditate and work on his feelings of self-worth and abundance. The next day, his business phone started to ring off the hook and continued to do so.

Right and Left Brain

The right and left sides of the brain control the opposite sides of the body. There are also physical and emotional differences between the right and left sides. The following chart outlines some of these characteristics as they relate to each side of the brain:

RIGHT BRAIN	LEFT BRAIN
Controls left side of body Intuitive thinking Artistic	Controls right side of body Logical thinking Practical

In order to have balance in everyday life, it is beneficial to have some sort of balance between right-and-left-brain stimulation. Many of my patients have found benefits in their overall health, from balancing activities from both sides of the brain. For instance, someone who predominantly uses his or her left brain as an accountant would become balanced by using the right brain for painting or sculpting.

Men and women differ in the way that their brains are wired. Men seem to use either one side of the brain or the other when doing a task. Women have more connections through the corpus callosum, which separates the right and left sides of the brain. Due to this difference, women can use both sides of the brain at once, hence, the ability to be better multi-taskers than men. I am generalizing, because we know that there are certainly some men who are fantastic multi-taskers, and some women have difficulty doing more than one thing at once.

Successful people typically have to think of many things at once. In business, it is important to be creative (right-brain), and logical (left) at the same time. For this reason, it is best to exercise both sides of the brain as much as possible, to be able to make business decisions from practical, yet creative standpoints.

Mind/Spirit Connection and Manifestation of Disease or Health

In my first year at naturopathic college, everyone was trying to teach us about the body/mind/spirit connection and its importance in health. I adopted the concept, but never understood what the spirit had to do with anything related to physical health. What I have come to learn is that the spiritual aspect of our being is the root of all. When our spirit is happy and fulfilled, our mind and body are healthy and free from illness.

The way we think affects the way our cells function. The more positive our thoughts, the more efficient our cells work to metabolize and excrete toxins. The more negative our thoughts, the less likely our cells work to reduce their toxic load. Negative-thinkers produce more illness for themselves than positive thinkers. It is very difficult to heal fully, without healing the spiritual aspects that lead to our ill health in the first place.

Clearing Toxic Emotions

Some emotions can be considered toxic, if they are repeatedly experienced. Emotions such as anger, resentment, jealousy, hatred, disappointment, fear and betrayal can all be harmful to your body, mind and spirit if they are felt for a period of time that lasts longer than what I call the "therapeutic emotional window." It is healthy to feel anger if someone or an event has caused the anger. What is more important is letting the anger go as quickly as it came into your consciousness. This is the therapeutic emotional window of opportunity. To harbour the anger for longer than is required to process it fully is deleterious to your physical, emotional and spiritual health. These stored emotions are toxic. I cringe when patients tell me they have been angry with the same person for twenty years. I know that many of the physical complaints they experience are probably associated with the stored toxic emotions. Naturally, part of the detoxification process is to clear these toxic emotions.

Exercises to clear toxic emotions

1. Journaling

- Write down all the emotions you are feeling that are disturbing your peace of mind
- Categorize the emotions, linking them to a particular person or event
- Rank the emotions, from most disruptive to least disruptive for your well-being
- Starting with the least disruptive, decide how you can let it go:
  i. Letting go via a conversation with the person who hurt you
  ii. Letting go by conversing with someone who will empathize with you
  iii. Letting go by writing a letter (that you don't necessarily have to send) to someone or even to yourself
  iv. Letting go through meditation
  v. Letting go with a prayer.
  vi. Letting go with the help of an energy healer.

- Move to the most disruptive emotions, following the same practice as above

Aside: You may find that a group of the toxic emotions are all linked to the same event or person. The good news is that they can all be cleared at once, in this case, usually through forgiveness.

2. Get out the punching bag

Physically letting out anger and frustrations in a healthy way is not only therapeutic for the mind, but can be physically beneficial. So, join a kickboxing class at your local gym, or use a simple pillow at home to let out your emotions in the privacy of your own home.

The Effects of Stress

There are very few aspiring or accomplished millionaires who haven't experienced a good amount of stress. Stress causes a vicious cycle that affects our well-being. Stress causes us to feel uprooted and ungrounded, which causes us to feel more stress, and the cycle continues. Stress causes us to disconnect from what is important in our daily lives, such as proper diet, exercise and sleep. When we are stressed, we are less likely to take care of our emotional and spiritual health as well.

I can't think of anyone that I know who doesn't have stress. Unless you are an extremely enlightened person or a Buddhist monk, you have stress. It is a natural part of our existence as humans on earth. We have work stress, or no-work stress, family stress, health stress, wealth stress or lack of wealth stress ... stress, stress, stress! So, we all have it, but it's what we do with it that makes all the difference. Studies show that if we have an outlet for stress, the deleterious effects of it are less than if we just store it. In the book *Why Zebras Don't Get Ulcers*, the author, Robert M. Sapolsky, talks about an experiment done on rats to test their stress levels. Two groups of rats were given shocks. One group was allowed to gnaw on some wood and the other was not. Guess what? The rats that were able to gnaw and had an outlet for stress formed fewer ulcers, compared with the other group with no outlet.

Stress has to be the number one cause of illness today. Stress is toxic. Stress has been studied extensively and is known to have certain physiological effects on the body. The following is a very simplified breakdown of the bodily effects of stress.

Stress causes part of the autonomic (automatic) nervous system to go into overdrive. This is called the sympathetic nervous system and causes:

- Increased respiration
- Increased heart rate
- Increased blood flow to the internal organs
- Increased blood pressure
- Decreased digestion in the small intestine
- Increased motility (movement) in the large intestine

The sympathetic drive is also known as the fight-or-flight response. It is a survival mechanism that allows the body to react to what it perceives as danger. The reaction in most animals is to run away from the stress. What is interesting is that even our everyday, non-threatening stressors can cause the same physiological mechanisms to fall into place – just as a hungry lion was chasing us.

Hans Selye was the father of the concept of stress and its physiological effects on the body. He developed the classification of the stress response and named it the general adaptation syndrome (GAS). Arousal is the first stage of the stress response. This is when the body prepares to fight. There is an increase in adrenalin and noradrenalin and cortisol, secreted by the adrenal glands. The next stage is the adaptation stage, when the body secretes sustained high levels of cortisol and alarm molecules. In this stage, there is altered glucose tolerance, blood pressure irregularities, thyroid and sex hormone changes. The final stage is exhaustion, when the cortisol levels drop, immunity is compromised, and chronic disease sets in.

What is common in today's society is that we push ourselves for prolonged periods of time, and usually have the energy to get whatever it is we are working on getting accomplished. However, we tend to get sick during our down time, or the holidays. This is a beautiful example of the GAS. The stress of a project keeps our cortisol, epinephrine and norepinephrin secretion high and in the adaptation stage. When the project is finished, we reach exhaustion and can get sick, because our hormone secretion will no longer sustain our needs.

Stress Causes Illness

Some people suffer from physical ailments due to stress alone. I had a patient, Joanna, whose chief complaint was migraine headaches. She had suffered from intense pain almost daily, for the past three years. She kept a log of the frequency and severity of her headaches. When I looked at the frequency of her most intense headaches, I realized that they were always on a Monday. I asked her if she liked her job. She said she liked her job but hated her boss. When I pointed out that her headaches were always most severe at the beginning of the working week, she opened up about the problems she had with working for her unsympathetic and demanding superior. It was as if a light bulb went off in her head in regards to her symptoms. I told her I could give her plenty of remedies and change her diet, but I believed that she would only be completely free of headaches once she dealt with her boss or quit her job.

Joanna took my advice and confronted her boss. She let him know her honest feelings. To her surprise, he apologized, saying that he hadn't realized that he was so hard on her. She was then able to let go of any resentment she had towards him. Her headaches disappeared and never came back!

Adrenal Gland Stimulation and Burnout

The adrenal glands are the stress glands, and secrete their hormones according to the amount of stress a person undergoes. Two important adrenal hormones are cortisol and dehydroepiandosterone (DHEA). They are produced by the adrenal cortex from cholesterol.
(See diagram)

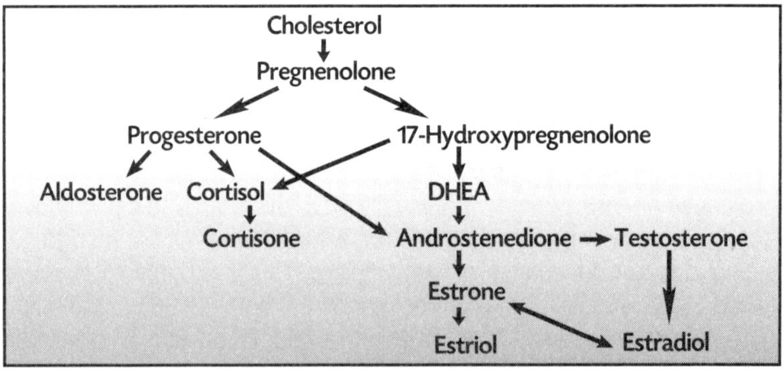

The secretion of cortisol is regulated by the circadian sleep-wake cycle. The largest cortisol secretion is first thing in the morning, around eight, followed by a gradual decrease for the rest of the day. Around midnight, the secretion is the lowest. The diurnal secretion of cortisol explains why many of us have a slump in energy in the afternoon. This is when the cortisol secretion is levelling out after its morning peak.

Symptoms of prolonged stress include insulin resistance, loss of sex-drive, central obesity and increased abdominal fat, loss of muscle tone, increased blood cholesterol, trigylcerides and blood pressure, insomnia, fatigue and depression.[37]

Adrenal Profile

The following is a questionnaire that lists the main signs and symptoms a person may experience if the adrenal glands have been overstressed and are now functioning at a lower than normal rate.

For each symptom described, score one if you have had it in the past, two if it occurs sometimes, three if it occurs often, and four if the symptoms are frequent and a major concern. (To make life easy, you can circle the number beside the symptom).

1	2	3	4	Symptoms present since stressful event (e.g., accident, death of loved one, pregnancy, break-up, etc.)	1	2	3	4	Nervousness
1	2	3	4	Prolonged exposure to stress	1	2	3	4	Dizziness on rising from a lying position
1	2	3	4	Environmental sensitivities	1	2	3	4	History of asthma or bronchitis
1	2	3	4	Food allergies	1	2	3	4	Hemorrhoids
1	2	3	4	Low energy, fatigue	1	2	3	4	Varicose veins
1	2	3	4	Other endocrine gland imbalances, e.g., thyroid	1	2	3	4	Arthritis, bursitis, joint problems
1	2	3	4	Anxiety attacks	1	2	3	4	Increased skin pigmentation
1	2	3	4	Excessive perspiration	1	2	3	4	History of drug use
1	2	3	4	Excessive urination	1	2	3	4	Consumption of refined foods, sugar
1	2	3	4	Muscle twitching	1	2	3	4	Use of coffee
1	2	3	4	Heart palpitation	1	2	3	4	Use of cigarettes
1	2	3	4	Eyes sensitive to light	1	2	3	4	Frequent colds
1	2	3	4	Edema of extremities	1	2	3	4	Aching calves
1	2	3	4	Crave salt	1	2	3	4	Weak ankles
1	2	3	4	Recurrent infections	1	2	3	4	Tired feet
1	2	3	4	Blurred vision	1	2	3	4	Low back pain
1	2	3	4	Headaches	1	2	3	4	Knee problems

A score of fifty or more indicates hypoadrenal function.

It is very common for successful people to score high on this questionnaire. Adrenal exhaustion is one of the most common ailments of my millionaire patients. The good news is that it is fairly easy to treat with naturopathic remedies and lifestyle changes..

How Stress Affects the Thyroid Gland

The thyroid gland is part of the endocrine system, and is responsible for maintaining our metabolism, energy and body temperature. The thyroid gland is located at the lower end of the front of the neck.

Stress has a direct effect on the function of the thyroid gland. During stress, the hypothalamus in the brain increases the production of corticotropin-releasing hormone, which indirectly inhibits the secretion of TSH from the pituitary. TSH is responsible for stimulating the thyroid to function.[38]

Symptoms of hypothyroidism or a low thyroid are the following:

- Cold body temperature
- Cold hands and feet
- Fatigue
- Night sweats
- Inability to lose weight easily
- Hair falling out
- Dry skin
- Swelling in neck

Note: Your medical doctor may check your blood for thyroid function and everything could appear normal, when, in fact, you may still have a low functioning thyroid gland. The body is very good at maintaining homeostasis and can keep the blood levels in the normal range when the thyroid is not functioning optimally. A naturopathic doctor will check your basal body temperature and do other tests, to determine if you have an under-active thyroid.

Stress and the Immune System

Chronic stress depletes our immune system. High levels of cortisol lower T-killer cells halt the maturing of white blood cells, and can even kill white blood cells directly. High cortisol is a protective mechanism in times of acute stress. If you were about to be ravaged by a hungry bear, your body's first instinct should not be to fight off the bacteria that you just encountered from swimming in the polluted lake. The body would use all its energy to get your body moving to get out of there – and fast. However, if the stress is prolonged and chronic, the elevated cortisol levels suppressing the immune system become more of a problem.

Stress and Digestion

In order to digest food properly, our systems need to be in relaxed mode, or parasympathetic branch of the autonomic nervous system. In this state, we secrete the enzymes necessary for digestion. For this reason, it is not advisable to eat on the run, in our cars, standing up, during heated family discussions, or in loud, chaotic atmospheres. We need to become more conscious of our food as nourishment and take the time and effort to create soothing atmospheres in which to eat and digest.

I always ask patients with digestive problems the circumstances in which they eat their meals. I am usually not surprised to find that most of them eat on the run. By slowing down and taking the proper time to enjoy meals, these patients often improve their digestion without taking any remedies at all. This is a great example of one of the principles of naturopathic medicine I mentioned in the introduction. By treating the root cause of disease, the symptoms will clear. If these patients just took digestive enzymes to improve their digestion, sure, their digestion would improve, yet it would only be a band-aid on the original problem – dysregulation of enzyme secretion due to stress.

Stress and Blood Sugar Regulation

High cortisol levels due to stress make it more difficult for the body to maintain blood glucose levels. Insulin receptor sites on cell walls become resistant to insulin when cortisol is high. This is called insulin resistance. The body reacts to too much glucose in the blood by secreting more insulin.[39] This eventually leads to type II diabetes, if not controlled. A yo-yo scenario can occur, in which one may be constantly munching on food to maintain one's blood sugar. This, of course, can lead to weight gain – causing more stress!

Tips on how to Combat Stress

Avoiding things that cause us stress

If something stresses you out, stop doing it! It is so simple, yet we tend to stay stuck in patterns that do not serve us well. By simply stopping or altering our behaviours, we can effectively cut down our stress load.

Stop procrastinating
Leave not until tomorrow, what can be done today.

We cause ourselves undue stress, because we delay doing things that need to be done. The delay itself causes stress, because it adds days (or weeks or months) to the dread of doing what will eventually get done anyway. If we take care of the task in a reasonably short time, the stress is reduced because it is not compounded over time.

Whenever we leave things to the last minute, there is often some unforeseen event that makes getting the task completed that much more difficult, and stressful. Planning and preparation are very helpful at keeping our stress levels down. Unfortunately, many of us need the last-minute stress to motivate us to do the work.

Meditation
An ancient remedy for stress, meditation is gaining popularity these days because it is easy to do anywhere. Meditation has been proven to reduce the risk of heart disease and stroke; it decreases pain and high blood pressure, and enhances the immune system.

Meditation is often practised at the end of yoga classes, and that may be an easy way to adopt it into your routine. Some people find it easier to meditate in a group rather than by themselves. The group setting in a quiet room allows you to stay focused on the meditation longer than you may be able to manage on your own. Meditation can be difficult at first – especially quieting the mind long enough to block out the thoughts of the day. With practise, it becomes easier to acquire a relaxed state, and the mind's chatter ceases.

Exercise
Exercise is one the most beneficial ways to combat stress. It has the added benefit of detoxifying and strengthening the body as well as alleviating stress. The type of exercise chosen should be very specific to the individual to the maximize benefits. For instance, if you work in a high-paced job with a lot of running around, a quieter type of exercise, such as yoga, would be more beneficial to ease your stress than a high-impact aerobic class. For others with more sedentary lifestyles, a more active type of exercise may suit them better for stress relief.

CHAPTER 9 | RELATIONSHIPS

No Meeting is by Chance

Every person that crosses your path does so for a reason. The relationships that you form with others are the building blocks of your life lessons. People who are closest to you will teach you the most about yourself. They will press buttons that no others can press. There are different degrees of relationships – from very intimate to passers-by – and even the person who checks out your groceries is there for a reason in your life. When you start to pay more attention to these people, you start to appreciate the wisdom in the Universe, and what it has in store for you.

In business, everyone that you encounter along the way is there for a reason. Whether you choose to do business with some people or not, they were brought to you for a specific reason. Most affluent people would agree that it is "who you know, not what you know" that makes the difference between success and failure in business. The more aware you become as to your power to attract the perfect people in your life to achieve your financial goals, the more you cherish every relationship you encounter along the way.

I like to think of life as a play in which I am one of the actors. I am connected to every other actor that is in the play in some way. I do not know all of the actors yet with whom I will be working in this lifetime, but they have all been chosen already by the director; the Creator. The director has a reason for introducing me to each and every person who floats in and out of the play. This analogy helps me when I am troubled by some of the people I have contact with. I see every meeting with another human as a gift and an opportunity to learn something about myself in the process of the interaction – be it a positive or negative experience.

In romantic relationships, we need to remind ourselves that the reason we are with our partners or lovers is to ultimately become better human beings. Unfortunately, many of us have the impulse to run away from relationships when the going gets tough. I once had lunch with a friend of mine and we were discussing a homeopathic case in which a man wanted to move away from his life and start over. My friend said, "You can't run away from yourself," which has stuck in my memory to this day. In relationships, we make it seem that we want to run away from our partners, but, in fact, it is an attempt to run away from the traits that we do not like in ourselves.

Unconditional Love

We need to commit ourselves unconditionally to our loved ones. That means to love without expectation or judgment. We can only be truly in love when we let go of conditions that become attached to that love. A good example of unconditional love is Nancy, who recently found out that her son was gay. Nancy never thought for a moment that this would change her loving relationship with her son. She was shocked by the news, but she didn't go a day without loving her son the same as she did when she thought he was heterosexual. When we attach conditions to our love like, "I will love you more if you change," or, "I will show you more affection if you come home earlier," we do not love freely. We love with the expectation of getting something in return. We need to give love without any expectation of it being reciprocated. The likelihood of being loved in return is quite high, but we can't expect it. I need to also say, that this doesn't mean that because we love unconditionally it gives others the right to step all over us. We still need to have boundaries in life. To allow others to take advantage of us is not a healthy scenario either.

If you have ever fallen in love with another person, you may have experienced the blissful time at the beginning of your relationship when everything about the other person was absolute perfection. The commencement of a romantic relationship is a good example of unconditional love. We all have faults. When we first fall in love with another person, these faults don't seem to matter as much as they do as time goes on. When we first fall in love, our hearts are open and give unconditionally. Later, our egos enter into the picture and start to find fault in our once-perfect mates. It is the ego and fear that move us away from unconditional love. When we reconnect with our spirits, it is easier to love unconditionally – without any expectations or conditions on love.

How to Detoxify the Negative Patterns in Relationships

We can all probably relate to having the same argument over and over again with someone we love. At some point, we need to let it go and move on. The constant struggle to achieve peace around an issue that doesn't resolve is a waste of time and energy. I once heard Dr. Wayne Dyer say, "Sometimes it is better to be kind than it is to be right." Arguments can also cause an accumulation of negative energy in our body, which over time can lend itself to illness. Therefore, it is important to detoxify these patterns for good. Some people find the answers they are looking for from counselling. Others find that if they learn to communicate properly, these issues clear up. A few tips are as follows:

a) Only discuss "the issues" when you are not angry
b) State the facts from your perspective
c) State your feelings/emotions on the matter
d) Decide on a mutually agreeable solution to the problem, if possible

Problems that occur in relationships often have nothing to do with the other person. The people with whom we fight are usually reflections of parts of ourselves that we do not like. So, if you think of it this way, is it not futile to constantly beat yourself up about the same issue? You cannot change other people. You can only change yourself and your actions in life. The next time the same negative pattern repeats in your relationship, change your reaction. If you keep doing the same thing and expect a different result, you will wait forever. If you heal your negative patterns, the relationship issues disintegrate.

And remember, there is no problem without a solution – no matter how impossible it may seem.

Creating Healthy Boundaries in Relationships

Someone once told me that in a romantic, lifelong relationship, the partners are like tall trees growing side by side. They gain strength from the proximity and energetic connection to each other, without allowing their branches to lean on the other tree. This is a great metaphor for relationships in that we need to be strong in ourselves, maintain our individuality, and avoid leaning too much on our mates. It is important not to let ourselves smother the other person, or be smothered or taken advantage of by the ones we love. The same is true not only for romantic relationships, but for any relationship we have with another human being. The way to ensure that these lines are not crossed is to create healthy boundaries in our relationships.

Creating healthy boundaries means discerning what is okay and not okay in the way we are treated, and how much we are willing to give of ourselves. When we have healthy boundaries, it is easy for us to voice our willingness to help others, or to be helped, to an extent that doesn't disrupt our sense of emotional, physical and spiritual balance. However, when we have difficulty defining our boundaries with others, we end up resenting ourselves and those who abuse our time and energy for their own good.

It is easy to appreciate the importance of having boundaries with children. Just as certain behaviours of children are acceptable and others are not, the same is true in our relationships with other adults. We need to voice our limits and boundaries with everyone in our lives.

Many of us do not exercise our right to say, "No." "No" is the best boundary builder that helps to keep our energy. Saying no is not derogatory or neglectful. It is merely a way to protect ourselves from doing more than we are meant to. People-pleasers have difficulty saying no because helping others is a way to boost their self-esteem. However, it is better to have self-esteem from within, rather than based on a condition of helping others. Unfortunately, people who do not set healthy boundaries are often lacking energy because they are using so much of their own energy helping others that they have little left for themselves. They then become resentful because they have no time or energy left – when they created the whole scenario in the first place by not setting boundaries. I see a lot of patients who are physically sick because they did not set boundaries with other people.

CASE study

Sherie, a fifty-seven-year-old woman, came to see me for digestive problems, fatigue and hormonal imbalance. She admitted being stressed out. She was a family person and took care of everyone – including her ex-husband! I gave her some remedies to balance her nervous system, improve her thyroid function and detoxify her system. For her follow-up visit, she reported no great improvement in any of her symptoms. I explained that if she didn't set some boundaries for her relationships, she would continue to tax her own body, mind and spirit. The next time I saw Sherie, she told me that she was able to say no to people who were trying to pull her in too many directions. Miraculously, her digestion and hormones improved, and she had loads of energy.

Resentment

Resentment builds when feelings are not discussed openly and frequently. We become resentful of our partners over time. Resentment survives only if we consciously feed it the negative energy and thought patterns on which it thrives. Resenting someone is toxic. It is an emotion that will drain your energy and eventually lead to more and more misery. The sooner we can stop resenting others, the sooner we can move on with our lives in a positive way.

Communication in the key to letting our loved ones know exactly what is going on in our little heads – whether it is nonsense or not. Many of our thoughts are fear-based when we resent someone or something. Women resent their husbands for working too much and not being around for the kids. Men resent women for not contributing as much to financial burdens. These are gross generalizations, yet very prevalent none the less. If the people we resent understand our frustration and fears, they may be able to help us come up with solutions to the underlying problems. Unfortunately, if left unchecked, resentment can build and build and become an enormous negative taint on a once loving and caring relationship.

In terms of affluence, resenting people from the past for whatever they may have done to you only holds you prisoner. Not being able to forgive someone who may have done you wrong in business only limits your ability to prosper with future endeavours. If you may be struggling financially, or business isn't where you would like it to be, ask yourself who you may be resenting and who do you need to forgive.

Relationships and Disease

I gave a lecture to a women's group about naturopathic medicine for female-related complaints. At the end of the session, I offered to demonstrate craniosacral therapy on a member of the audience. I chose a woman, based on my own intuition, out of the large number of attendees who wanted to volunteer. The woman lay down on the treatment table and told us that she had a constant headache every day for the past twenty years. I asked her what had happened twenty years ago. She said she got married. The audience chuckled. The woman was in tears. Without having to delve deeper into her history, I already knew that her headaches had much to do with her relationship and marriage.

Relationships do not cause disease. It is our inability to see and then learn the lessons we are meant to learn in our relationships that can cause our bodies to become ill.

The people that are closest to us in our relationships are our mirrors in life. They reflect back to us our good and bad personality traits. The things that you like the least in the people closest to you are the things you often like least about yourself. Read that sentence again. So, when you repeatedly have an issue with someone, you need to open your eyes upon yourself to see what it is that needs to be healed inside you.

You may have heard that the most difficult relationships you have will teach you the most. We intuitively choose people to be in our lives for very distinct reasons. Our whole purpose for being here is to become better human beings. We cannot do this effectively without having relationships with others that teach us what we need to learn to further us along our spiritual paths. If you have major problems with some people in your life, see them as a blessing, because they will likely teach you the most about becoming a better person.

CASE study

Lisa, a twenty-five-year-old patient, was depressed over the loss of her three-year relationship with her boyfriend. I happened to see her a few months after the break-up. She was still grieving. I asked her how the relationship was. She said her boyfriend was quiet, non-communicative, jealous, lacked self-esteem, and was unfaithful. I asked her if she learned anything about herself in the course of the relationship. Her eyes lit up and she said she learned she was stronger than she thought, because she finally had the strength to break up with him. Lisa went on to say that she was intelligent, beautiful, ambitious, and ready to find another boyfriend if it was in the cards for her.

Lisa was able to see her positive and negative traits, because she put herself in a relationship that would teach her these things. The old saying, "It is better to have loved and lost, than never to have loved at all," is very true.

Giving up Judgment

How many times have you had a fight with someone in which you put them down to make yourself feel better or more powerful? We get ourselves into power struggles, when we do not have the self-esteem to see above and beyond the everyday issues. When we judge others and verbally attack them, we are only displaying our own lack of self-esteem. If we truly love ourselves, there is no reason to put someone down – no matter what they have done to hurt our feelings. If someone has made a mistake, they have probably already told themselves at least ten times how stupid they are inside their own head. Most of us know when we are in the wrong, and we are our own worst critics. Further judgment and criticism from others around us adds salt to the wound, and adds to the negative emotions, which are already floating around in our systems. Again, these negative thought patterns are toxic and can lead to ill health. So, the next time you have the urge to attack someone verbally for their faults, hold back and ask yourself what you can do to help their situation, instead of making it even worse.

We like to think that we are right and others are not. We judge others because of their differences. In fact, the differences we see in others are usually things we either admire in them or they reflect back to us things that we dislike about ourselves. Whenever I have problems with others, I ask myself: Why is their behaviour so irritating to me, and what it is that I can relate to in their behaviour, which I see in myself?

Giving up the Need to Control

When we feel we have lost control of our own lives, we look to find control in other areas. We may try to control those around us, to attain some level of power for ourselves. The people we try to control the most include our children, our spouses, and our siblings and sometimes even our parents – retribution, I guess, for all those years of feeling like powerless children. As a parent, I have found there is a fine line between guidance and control. We like to have things run a certain way, some of us more than others. If we can allow our loved ones to be individuals, but, at the same time, direct them when they need guidance – or even better, when they ask for it – we would have healthier relationships.

Society has conditioned us to be strong and independent. But we also need to be vulnerable sometimes, and to ask others for help when we need it. If we have more faith and allow our destiny to unfold, there is less need to control anything in our lives – whether it is our own life, or the lives of our loved ones.

The more we try to control, the less control we have. I have seen many patients who are having difficulty with their teenage children. The parents do their best to protect and guide the teenagers, but have a controlling manner of doing so. Naturally, the teenagers rebel, and both they and their parents become frustrated with each other's behaviour. Parents can learn to give guidance without the influence of their own hopes and dreams for their children. The children will be more willing to listen to guidance than they will to control.

When we attempt to control, it shows our extreme lack of faith. Everything will always work out in the end. The more we learn to go with the flow, rather than controlling others' behaviour, the easier our relationships become. The less friction in a relationship, the less stress we experience in our lives in general; and less stress means better health.

Sex

Relationships need to be healthy on all levels – physically, emotionally, and spiritually. Physical health in a relationship, for most couples, means having a healthy sexual relationship. Sex involves the body, mind and spirit. Healthy sex is important and may be somewhat downplayed by medical practitioners. When was the last time your doctor asked you how your sex life was? Naturopathic doctors are trained to ask these questions, as they are pertinent to one's overall health and well-being.

Sex is a celebration of the love that two people share for each other. Sex is a beautiful way to bond with another, especially at the soul level. When naturopathic doctors ask about a patient's sex life, it usually gives us an indication as to how healthy the relationship is between partners, which has a huge impact on one's day-to-day health.

Sex provides a non-verbal communication between two lovers. The positive energy that is exchanged between partners during sexual intercourse has a direct effect on the chakras and energetic balance of these energy centres. When the chakras are balanced, the whole body, mind and spirit are in synch. Mary, a woman in her late fifties, told me she was convinced her health and energy was so good at her age because of her active sex life with her husband. Most people who enjoy sex with their loved ones feel good afterwards, and when you feel good, you feel healthy.

Napoleon Hill, in his brilliant book *Think and Grow Rich*, declared that a strong, positive sexual energy was important to attract affluence into one's life. He stated that certain individuals have a strong sexual attractiveness that helps others desire to do business with them. He also stated that if you are able to channel your own sexual energy in a productive way, it can propel your business and create more affluence.[40]

Mental/Emotional Health in Relationships

Mental/emotional health in a relationship is paramount. If you are not emotionally happy with your partner, the relationship suffers. Emotions run high between lovers, and there are fluctuating emotional ebbs and flows of closeness and togetherness versus distance and solitude. It is unrealistic for loved ones to be together and everything to be hunky-dory every day of their lives. We are meant to have differences with our partners. This is how we learn. This is how we mature in the relationship. When we are close, we need to cherish the time we have together. However, when we hit the rough spots in a relationship, we need to be able to step out of the situation and take a look at what we are meant to learn. The rough times are not fun, but a necessity in learning how to relate to another human being on emotional grounds.

The people we choose as our lovers or life partners have a knack for pushing our buttons in exactly the right way to knock us off our emotional balance. Have you ever woken up one morning and everything is going your way? The day ahead looks fantastic and you can't wait to step out into the world, then you are blindsided by an "issue" that creeps up between you and your partner? The "issue" affects the way you feel for the rest of the day, or even the whole week. When we become balanced in body, mind and spirit, we are less likely to be thrown from our equilibrium by those who press our buttons. We are able to look at the lesson to be learned, learn it, and then move on. A rough spot in our relationship may then only last a few hours, rather than a few days or weeks.

CASE study

Joe thought that his relationship with his wife, Nancy, was perfect. When asked to rate the relationship between one and ten, ten being fantastic, he said his relationship was a nine. Nancy, however, rated the relationship a five out of ten. Nancy was frustrated with her husband, because she noticed that he made his work a priority over time spent with her and their two children. Joe could not believe that Nancy did not understand that in order for him to provide for the family, he had to work long hours and be away from home. Nancy needed more emotional support from Joe, which was difficult to receive if he was never around.

I see this pattern in relationships time and time again. The man believes he is doing everything right because he is providing financial support for the family unit. However, financial support is only one of the factors in a healthy relationship on the physical level. Women and men need emotional support and a spiritual connection, in order for the relationship to work long term.

CHAPTER 10 | NATUROPATHIC REMEDIES FOR DETOXIFYING THE MIND

When we think of detoxification, we usually think about ways we may be able to cleanse our bodies. It seems unlikely to be able to detoxify the mind. Thankfully, naturopathic medicine offers some wonderful modalities that help to clear the mind of toxic thoughts and emotions.

Classical Homeopathy

Homeopathic remedies are helpful for healing mental patterns that are not conducive to a healthy way of life. Homeopathic remedies have the ability to stop negative thought patterns and fears in someone, when the correct remedy is given. Homeopathic remedies are very precise in their characteristics and only work properly when the exact remedy in the exact potency or dilution is given at precisely the right time in a person's life. There are over five thousand different homeopathic remedies derived from a plant, animal or vegetative source. Remedies work not only on the emotional sphere, but on the physical and spiritual as well. Homeopathic remedies are best prescribed by a practitioner who is trained in classical homeopathy. However, the following sketches of common prescriptions of homeopathic remedies for the mental/emotional complaints of a patient can be used. If a remedy fits someone's personality, you are able to read it and say, 'Wow, that sure describes him or her.'

Natrum muriaticum

(Sea salt)

- Major grief remedy
- Shuts down or gets sick after an emotional loss or suffering, for example, after the death of a loved one, break-up of a relationship
- Prefers to be alone when upset
- Very sensitive
- Responsible
- Unable to cry even though very sad
- Depressed
- Hardworking, perfectionist
- Never late, always on time
- Fears: Robbers, claustrophobia, dark, storms, insects, germs, heights

Pulsatilla
(Windflower)

- Weepy, changeable moods
- Timid, shy
- Complaints move from place to place, for example, one day knee pain, next day shoulder pain, next day headache
- Insecure, asks, "Do you love me?"
- Feels better if consoled
- Fears: heights, claustrophobia, insanity, dark, robbers, mirrors
- Feels forsaken
- Jealousy
- Easily influenced by others

Lycopodium

- Insecure
- Fear of commitment
- Lack of self-control or discipline. For example, will eat junk food in excess, even though he or she knows it is not good for them
- Bully, arrogant behaviour to those with less authority
- Anxious about health, finances, career
- Stage fright
- Fears: ghosts, claustrophobia, public speaking, cancer, being alone at night

Nux Vomica

- Type A personality
- Workaholics
- Addicted to coffee, cigarettes
- Work all day, can't sleep at night because they worry about work tomorrow
- Irritable, especially towards their family members
- Impatient

Lachesis
(Bushmaster snake)

- Jealous
- Sarcastic
- Unpredictable
- Can be rude, lash out when angry
- Talkative, loquacious
- Fears: snakes, poison, heart disease, insanity, vomiting
- Avoid wearing things around the neck

- Symptoms appear on the left side of body
- Craves alcohol, alcoholism
- PMS, irritable, jealous, depressed, hot flashes, headache
- Very sexual people

Sepia

(Cuttlefish ink)

- Usually a female remedy
- Irritable
- Sarcastic
- Separates self from family members
- Overwhelmed housewives
- Hormonal imbalances, PMS, menopause
- Craves chocolate, vinegar, sweets, bread
- Bearing down pains, as if the organs would drop out of the body
- Aggravation from giving birth

Phosphorus

- Outgoing
- Friendly
- Lively
- Has a "spark" to their personality
- "Jumpy," can startle easily
- Clairvoyant, intuitive
- Feels worse when alone
- Ungrounded
- Fears: thunderstorms, being alone, dark, death, ghosts, insects, natural disasters
- When sick, loses "spark" and is more reclusive

Aurum

(Gold)

- Great depression, suicidal states
- Egotistical
- Serious
- Outbursts of anger
- Feels better with music
- Spiritually inclined
- He is the "king" in his mind

Calcarea carbonica

- Slow, shy personality

- Puts up a shell on the exterior so others do not really see who he/she is
- Can be physically round, overweight
- Craves ice cream, milk, sweets, eggs
- Feels overwhelmed
- Stubborn

Sulfur

- Selfish individuals
- Quick-tempered
- Lack of care for personal appearance, cleanliness
- Sensitive to any nasty odour but does not notice his own body odour
- Fears: heights, failure, disease, claustrophobia[41]

Herbal Medicine

Herbal medicine can be used to balance out mental stress and negative thought patterns. Herbs have a pharmacological effect and can alter the brain chemistry. Herbal remedies are best when taken for short amounts of time. I usually discourage the constant use of herbs, because they do not cure the problem at hand, but merely make life more tolerable, while other mental work is done to clear toxic patterns of thinking. The following herbs are helpful for depression and anxiety:

St. John's wort - *(Hypericum perforatum)*
Part used: Aerial part
Actions: Anti-inflammatory, astringent, vulnerary, nervine, anti-microbial

St. John's wort is a common prescription in natural medicine for depression. It can relieve anxiety and tension if taken in high enough doses. It is also used externally for bruises, varicose veins and mild burns.

Caution: Photosensitivity (sensitivity to light and sun). Not to be used at the same time as prescription antidepressants.

Valerian - *(Valeriana officinalis)*
Part used: Rhizome and roots
Actions: Sedative, nervine, hypnotic, central depressant, hypotensive

Valerian is a sedative that has a calming effect. It induces sleep

in those who suffer from anxious thoughts before bed that keep them awake. Valerian does not affect REM sleep, and allows the patient to still enjoy dreams.

Passion flower - *(Passiflora incarnata)*
Parts used: Whole plant
Actions: Nervine, hypnotic, anti-spasmodic, hypotensive

Passion flower is a calming herb that relaxes the nervous system. It induces a restful sleep without having a narcotic effect.[42]

Acupuncture
Acupuncture is considered a metal therapy in Chinese medicine. It can be helpful in draining earth energy, according to the five element theory. The five elements in Chinese medicine include fire, water, earth, metal and wood. When people have high earth energy, they may have anxiety. Acupuncture is used on specific points, suiting an individual's needs to balance excess earth energy.

Craniosacral Therapy
The mind can be instantly relaxed with craniosacral therapy. (See Chapter Ten: Naturopathic Remedies for Detoxifying the Mind; Craniosacral Therapy). The first step in a craniosacral treatment is usually called the still point. This move temporarily stops the secretion of the cerebrospinal fluid from the fourth ventricle of the brain. The autonomic nervous system then goes into the parasympathetic mode, or the more relaxed state. Unfortunately, many of us live our lives in the sympathetic state, or the fight-or-flight response. Physiologically, this has many deleterious effects on the body, if prolonged.
(See Chapter Eight).

I usually end my lectures with a demonstration of craniosacral therapy because I have found it so useful in my practice. A volunteer that I chose at a lecture said she hadn't slept properly in years. Her stress was high, and I had a sense that she was in the sympathetic, or stressed, mode for most of her life. I did the still point and she was asleep in seconds. I was quite shocked myself, but was happy to have demonstrated to the audience how effective the therapy was.

Counselling
Naturopathic doctors are counsellors for much of their time in practice. We have counselling as part of our curriculum at naturopathic college.

Most patients start to feel better by talking about their problems and by being heard. Naturopaths are often the link to the innermost emotional concerns of a patient, without the stigma of seeing a "shrink" or counsellor. Most naturopaths are very good at opening people up so that they can be more aware of how their emotional state affects their physical body. I don't know how many times I have been forewarned that a patient, who doesn't open up to anybody, would be a difficult case for me, and they ended up telling me their whole life story.

We all like to feel validated. Talking about our fears, hang-ups and negative patterns to someone else, such as a naturopath, allows us to be less judgmental towards ourselves. When we give up self-judgment, we give up toxic patterns of self-hatred and loathing, which deplete our self-esteem and ability to accomplish our goals.

Counsellors or naturopaths can only help a patient if they have done the work on themselves. There is a saying among health-care practitioners: "You can't take anyone further along than you have gone yourself." This is where it becomes very important when choosing a naturopath or counsellor that you think you may have a good rapport with. However, not all naturopaths choose to do a lot of counselling, which may appeal to you or not.

Breathing Exercises

Breathing exercises can be very helpful to clear the mind of toxic emotions. Proper breathing involves using the entire lung capacity. Most of us are chest breathers and only use the top third to half of our lungs. The complete breath, as described below, helps to use the entire lung and has many benefits:

- Encourages use of diaphragm and strengthens it
- Purifies and enriches the blood
- Strengthens the lungs and abdominal muscles
- Increases immune system function
- Calms the nervous system
- Increases oxygenation to all parts of the body

To do the complete breath exercise, follow the steps below for five to ten minutes at a time, twice a day if possible.

1. Sit up straight either in a chair with both feet on the ground or cross-legged on the floor.

2. Inhale slowly through the nose for a count of four, letting the abdomen expand and the ribs flaring outwards.
3. Hold the breath for one to five seconds.
4. Exhale slowly to the count of four until the lungs have emptied completely. The exhalation should not be a blowing action, merely the lungs recoiling to their original un-inflated state.
5. Repeat for another four to five cycles.

Meditation/Relaxation

Some of the best ways to clear the mind and detoxify busy thoughts and fears is through relaxation and meditation. Relaxation involves deep breathing and an awareness of the breath. Relaxation is usually done in a comfortable position, either sitting or lying down. The end of a yoga class is called the final relaxation, in which you allow the body to be still and the mind to concentrate on nothing. This is usually a lot easier said than done for most people. Yoga instructors often call the final pose the corpse pose, for final relaxation is the most difficult posture in yoga because you have to relax the body and the mind. Our heads are constantly full of little thoughts that crowd out the more important ones such as "Life is great," or "I love my life." Instead, we think about what to eat for dinner, when to pick up the kids from school, how we forgot to pay the hydro bill, etc.

Relaxation is about doing nothing and allowing the mind to rest. It is not the same as sleep – in which the mind is usually still active in the form of dreaming. Relaxation allows the entire body to recharge, like a battery. Rest for the mind is like exercise for the body, actually giving you more energy when you are finished. Relaxation in small intervals during a hectic day can really improve overall health. All you need is a quiet space and a few minutes to tune out the hustle and bustle of everyday life.

Meditation is similar to relaxation in that it allows for a down-regulation of thoughts, and a quiet space for the body to relax. Meditation can be more involved, because you can start to guide your spirit's awareness into lessons you are to learn. In meditation, you can ask questions to the Universe or your Higher Power, and gain answers that can direct you in your life. Meditation is not for everyone, but can be very helpful for those who do it frequently. There are various regimes for meditation that are too involved to elaborate on in the context of this book, but I encourage those who are interested to pursue meditation.

Patients often tell me that they cannot meditate because they can't turn off their minds. They give up on the process, because they think it is impossible to sit and think of nothing. It is just as if I told you: Do not think of the colour red. And what did you think of? If in meditation you tell your mind not to interrupt with the thoughts of the day, it will automatically think of them. Practice makes perfect. The more you practise meditation, the easier it becomes. I tell patients that if they can even think of nothing for one or two minutes, that is enough for meditation.

Visualization

Visualization is the use of positive visual stimuli in the imagination to create a tranquil atmosphere in which to relax. Visualization for many people involves picturing a scene that has a positive and relaxing effect on their body. The mind cannot think of negative thoughts when it is concentrating on the beautiful scene. Visualization can also be used as a therapeutic device, in which the patient pictures disease leaving his or her body, or cancer cells being eaten up by the cells of the immune system.

I created the following visualization to help people to relax and tune into their spiritual purpose on earth. You can record the visualization on to tape and play it back to yourself.

To be able to fully relax, perhaps light a candle in a darkened room during the visualization. Unplug your phones and create a quiet space, in which you will not be interrupted. I recommend that if you tape the following, you could play some relaxing music in the background. Read the visualization very slowly with breaks, as I have indicated in brackets.

Close your eyes and take a few deep breaths. Let the energy fill your lungs and enter through the top of your head, or your seventh chakra, as you inhale deeply. As you exhale, allow any negative or tense energy to leave your body effortlessly. Continue to breathe slowly, allowing the breath to fill the entirety of your lungs. **(Break)** *As you breathe, begin to focus on my voice, as it leads you on a wonderful journey to a special place where you feel your best.* **(Break)** *This place is sacred to you, and only you will be present in this place.*

Continue to breathe for a few moments now, bringing the breath down all the charkas: number seven at the top of the head, **(Break)** *number* *six at the level of the eyes,* **(Break)** *number five at the throat,* **(Break)** *number four at the chest or heart,* **(Break)** *number three at the lower part of the ribs,* **(Break)** *number two at the pelvic region,* **(Break)** *and number one at the base of the spine or the tailbone. Ground yourself and connect to the centre of the earth. We will continue in a few moments.* **(Break)**

Imagine yourself in your special and sacred place. Here you feel completely relaxed, in tune with your body, mind and spirit. **(Break)** *In this space, you are free to experience whatever you need to heal yourself.* **(Break)** *You feel completely at ease in your own being, bringing awareness to any areas that have tension or blocked energy.* **(Break)** *Using your breath, breathe in positive white light and healing energy into any areas with blockages.* **(Break)** *With the exhale, allow any negative or blocked energy and tension to leave your body with ease.*

Allow your body to give you any messages it may have for your well-being. **(Break)** *Allow the tranquillity of the moment to give your body the time and space needed to heal. In this sacred place, you feel at ease and one with your spirit. Your spirit is happy here and leaves all negativity, fear and judgment outside this place.* **(Break)**

Know that you can return to this place whenever you feel the need to. This space can be created in your mind at any time and any place for your healing, and to connect to your inner self. **(Break)**

Take a few more deep breaths and bring awareness to the way you feel in body, mind and spirit, allowing any leftover blockages of energy to leave your body effortlessly. (Break) When you are ready, slowly open your eyes and reconnect with your present surroundings. Ground yourself again through your root or first chakra, connecting your energy to the centre of the earth

I strongly recommend that you make sure you are back to your senses, before you get up and go about your business for the rest of the day. Take your time at the end of the visualization before you get up and move. I learned from one participant that after the first time he tried it, he drove home as if he were drunk. This is certainly possible, if you are not grounded after this type of exercise. Since then, I always ask my participants if they feel they've "come back" after visualizations – even though most of them would like to stay in their sacred place forever!

Exercise
Exercise is a fantastic way to clear the mind of negative thoughts. For some, exercise is a mere distraction from the thoughts that repeat in their heads. Exercise or participating in sports is usually a positive experience that allows the physical body to take over for a while, thus, letting the mind rest. In terms of releasing negative emotions, such as anger and frustration, I usually recommend a healthy exercise; say golf or tennis, in which you can use all of your pent-up energy to hit the ball harder or farther. A negative energy is transformed into a positive one, which is helpful in detoxification.

Prolonged exercise can cause a release of endorphins, which are hormones that make us feel good. Endorphins are the chemicals that cause a "runner's high."

Yoga
Yoga calms the mind because the focus becomes the breath and the postures. It is very difficult to continue to think our negative thoughts in the middle of a difficult yoga posture that requires balance, strength, flexibility and the proper breathing pattern. Yoga postures also divert blood flow either towards or away from the head, which is said to clear the mind of negative thoughts and energy.

CHAPTER 11 | THE DETOXIFICATION OF SPIRIT

The Importance of Spirit

Our spirit is our core. It's the part of us that is connected to everything else in the Universe. Our spirit will guide us when we listen to it, to accomplish what we are meant to during our stay on this planet. Our spirit is our foundation, and we have it for life. Our body may die and our mind goes with it, but our spirit is everlasting. If we take care of our spirits, we can live a joyful, pleasant and fulfilled life. If we learn to listen to what our spirit wants, we begin to realize that life can be the beautiful journey that God intended it to be for us. We've probably all heard the saying, "Let your spirit soar." If you set your spirit free, you will find it guides you to circumstances and possibilities that not even your mind could ever dream up. Spirit is oneness with God and the Universe. Your spirit takes care of you because it is a piece of God. Your spirit is your friend, your teacher and your connection to all that is.

Ego

The ego is the part of all of us that questions our faith. It is the part of us that condemns, compares and tries to outperform the works of our spirits. The ego gains its energy from judging others and trying to always win or be better than somebody else. The ego is the fault-finder. Where the spirit works in love, the ego works in fear. Our spirits are inherently filled with love, whereas our egos are filled with fear. However, our egos are necessary to keep the balance of good and bad in our bodies.

If we can learn to follow our spirits more than our ego, we will all lead more fulfilled and prosperous lives. The ego slows down our attaining greatness, because it perpetuates our fears. Fear motivates us in a negative way to achieve more for ourselves. On the other hand, love motivates us to do things for the right reason, and what is better for humankind.

Spirit and Religion

Spirituality is often confused with religion. One could debate this matter for years, and some have made it their life's work. In my opinion, religion means organized belief patterns and practices that follow the guidance of one or more authority figures, such as God. Spirituality to me means the belief that someone or something exists that has ultimate wisdom over all. Spirituality does not necessarily need to follow a doctrine or religion. For many, being a spiritual person means believing in a Higher Power.

Some people shy away from spiritual matters out of fear. They do not want to believe that some force other than their own actions can have control over their destiny. Others do not want to be one of those "religious types," because the stereotype of being connected to God includes Bible thumpers and preaching aloud to the heavens in the middle of a busy street. However, spirituality is a connection to everyone and everything. Living a spiritually fulfilled life is the most rewarding way to exist, because you are gently guided by a force that wants only the best for you.

Energy

Energy is everywhere and is everything. We all give off and accept energy. Energy can be positive or not so positive. Most of us can relate to intuitively picking up on someone's energy, without even speaking to him or her. We can walk into a room full of people and be drawn towards certain individuals and repelled by others. This is energy at work. All humans are given these intuitive abilities. Some of us are more in tune with them than others. Our intuition was given to us to protect and guide us on our paths to ultimate peace and happiness. When we learn to tap into our intuition and our inner voice, our lives change.

In medicine, the flow of energy affects the way our bodies work. For instance, if the electrical impulses of energy that stimulate the heart to beat are disrupted, the heart may not beat in a coordinated fashion, causing arrhythmia. Energy exists in subtler ways in the body, as well.

For instance, energy is present in the acupuncture meridians and can be manipulated with acupuncture needles. If the flow of energy is either too robust or too little in the acupuncture points, the practitioner can adjust it to a normal amount, with the correct technique.

The Human Energy Field or Aura

Our bodies have an energy field called the human energy field, or aura. The aura surrounds our entire body and extends about three and a half feet away from our skin. We can all see auras with our intuitive sense and third eye, whether we are conscious of it or not. We have all met someone for the first time, and either instantly liked them, disliked them, or were neutral in our feelings towards them without knowing why. This phenomenon occurs because we pick up the energy in their aura. For example, people who are very loving usually have a lot of positive energy in their astral body, or auric level. We intuitively pick up this positive energy that surrounds them.

In business, we may be attracted to certain people based on their aura or energy patterns. We may also be repelled by certain people's energy. This is a protective mechanism that our spirit has in order for us to avoid potentially negative experiences. So, when you get a bad vibe about someone, or about doing business with them, follow that instinct and go elsewhere. Similarly, if you get a good vibe about a person or situation, pursue it. Your intuition and ability to read people's energy will rarely lead you astray.

The aura has different levels or "bodies" associated with it, all representing different vibrations of energy. These auric levels are all associated with the seven chakras.[43]

Faith

Many of us have lost faith in a higher power, or have never even connected with it. The truth is that no prayer goes unanswered. Sometimes the prayer may not be answered in the way we expect it, or pray for, but it is always answered. "No" is sometimes the answer – whether we like it or not.

When we lose our faith in the natural order of life, we are continually reacting to life and situations, instead of merely flowing with them. We attempt to control other people, ourselves and the daily events in our lives. The more we try to control, the less power we have as spiritual beings.

We need to release the outcome of the future and any expectations we may have. What will be, will be. It is the journey towards our fate that is important. I struggled for a long time with expectations of myself and of others. Once I let go of expecting others to behave in a certain way, or for certain events to take place, I found a sense of peace and less stress. I became plugged into what I call the "FLOW" of the Universe, instead of always trying to swim against the current.

Having faith that the Creator will always take care of us is a freeing experience. It allows us to live day to day, without the fear of "what if?" So many of us live in the "what if?" mode, in which every possible outcome that we can predict in our heads is a disaster. Fear is a lack of faith and becomes toxic to our emotional, spiritual and eventually physical health.

People who suffer from panic attacks are often stuck in the "what if?" scenario. They most definitely lack faith and predict horrible outcomes, which they know they won't be able to overcome. The physical body literally breaks down and incapacitates these people during the panic attack. These patients usually improve immensely with homeopathics, which help to drain these toxic thoughts from the mind, as well as by learning to live in the present moment.

Live in the Present

In order to set our spirits free, we need to let go of the past and stop stressing about the future. Living in the present is the only way to live. As I once heard Deepak Chopra say, "The past is history, the future a mystery, the now is a gift, and that's why it's called the present."

If we start to decipher what we stress about, it is usually something from the past or the future. Rarely do we have stress in the present moment. This is why it is so important to stay in the present. We can only influence what is happening in the present. We can only be productive in the present. We can only make positive choices for our futures in the present.

In order to be truly happy in the present, one has to leave the past behind and not worry about the future. The past cannot be changed, as we all know. We can, though, bring to the present things that we have learned in the past and use those experiences to help us in the future. However, to dwell on past events, either positive or negative, is a waste of time and energy. Living in the past can keep our mind and spirit toxic. Part of detoxification of the entire mind, body and spirit is to let go. Without letting go, negative energy accumulates and can lead to disease.

The only thing that exists is the present. Einstein proved that everything is relative to the present moment. Life is lived in the present moment. You can only change things for yourself in the present moment.
I usually ask my patients – if they haven't already told me – if there is anything that they haven't cleared from their past. I find that people who are depressed usually either live in the past or the future. They dwell on past mistakes and fear making future mistakes.

We can be much more productive in our lives if we live in the present moment. Consider how much time we use in our heads thinking about the past or the future. If we converted this brain space into productivity in the present moment, we could all be so much more. Thoughts are distracting, especially negative thoughts about the past or future. They can also keep us stuck in the same patterns that keep us running on the treadmill of life and never getting anywhere.

I would like to clarify that it is still important to have dreams and ambitions for the future. However, do today whatever you can to make those dreams a reality. Every moment of every day is either a successful use of your energy or not. The more successful choices you make for yourself, the more successes you will enjoy in the future. Make every day count.

I think many of us forget that there is energy much greater than ourselves, which governs what will be (or not be) in our lives. I am not immune to having negative thoughts, even though I have come a long way in this department. When I am down and out, I always, at some point, remember that the Universe or God has a plan for me that is so great I cannot even fathom it in my mind. I also know that the less time I spend worrying about things, the more positive actions I will accomplish towards my ultimate destiny. Luckily, the same is true for everyone. Everyone is destined to greatness. It is the plan of the Universe. It is the ultimate plan. We just need to wake up and realize it for ourselves NOW, IN THE PRESENT MOMENT.

Exercise to let go of the past

Use a piece of paper to make a check mark each time you find yourself thinking about the past in a negative way. Be aware of how much time you spend thinking of the past each day. To change the behaviour, each time you think of the past, divert your thinking to something positive in the present. Repeat over and over again, continuing to check your page, each time you think of the past. With time, you will think less and less about the past.

I recommend reading *The Power of Now* by Eckhart Tolle, a fantastic book about the importance of living in the present moment.

Karma

Karma is the law of reciprocation. What we give, we get. If we give positive energy out into the Universe, positive things will come back to us. The same is true for negative energy. If we give out negative energy, negative energy will come back to haunt us. Newton's third law of motion states that for every action, there is an equal and opposite reaction. This is similar to karma. We will manifest for ourselves, exactly what we get. There is no escaping karma. It applies to everyone, all the time.

I am always reminded of karma whenever I throw away a piece of gum without wrapping it up properly and disposing of it in a trash bin. I know that within a couple of weeks, I will step on a fresh piece of gum, which will take me at least five minutes to remove from my shoe. This is karma – and it never fails. Karma can be used to our advantage or disadvantage. If we do and say positive things for other people, positive things will be done for us. However, if we lie, cheat and steal, we will also be lied to, cheated and stolen from. With karma, it doesn't necessarily mean that gestures, good or bad, will be reciprocated by the same person that we helped (or not). Karma means that the Universe will provide us with the same.

People blame illness on bad karma or bad luck. These folks need to realize that their illnesses or toxicity, probably go back to the way that they live. If people live in love, and not in fear, they generally have good karma. If they live in fear and negativity, they may not have as good karma.

Karma can be particularly helpful when it comes to finances. The most financially successful people that I have met have been extremely generous, even before they had financial success. They have learned that by giving, you receive.

When we start to pay attention to the way karma works, it is remarkable that even our thoughts can have a karmic effect. Thoughts are energy that we put out into our surroundings. Again, negative thoughts attract negative circumstances, whereas positive thoughts attract positive ones. I see karma at work when I drive. I do my best to let people pass in front of me when the need arises. I then see that other people allow my passage when I am in need of some space to go into a lane. Try it. You too will be able to see karma at work.

Give Up Judgment

To live a spiritually healthy life, we have to give up our need to judge others. Judgment is a toxic trait, and manifests negativity towards those who judge. We judge others so much that many of us don't even realize it. Judgment means forming a conclusion about someone or their behaviour based on our own reality. The judgment need not always be negative. We can judge people in a positive regard as well, but it is still a judgment. We may say, "Oh, she is so lucky to have so much money, she doesn't have a care in the world," when, in fact, the person we are judging may be miserable. Judgment is toxic. It conjures up the need to classify things as either good or bad. The bottom line is that things just are – period. People just are. However, sometimes such a simple way of living can be the most difficult task because we have to unlearn everything we thought was right until this point. Living a non-judgmental life means giving up racism, gender differences, religious differences, politics and so on, in order to allow our minds, bodies and spirits the time to do what we are meant to.

Judgment is so common because we seek to feel better about ourselves, no matter at what expense. Part of our ego drives us to judge others, to make them look worse than we are. The truth is, it is impossible to make ourselves better people by degrading others. To try to do so is a waste of precious time and energy, which could be spent making the world a better place.

Forgiveness

The greatest gift you can give yourself is forgiveness.

A good friend once told me that forgiveness is selfish. You do it for yourself and not for the person you are forgiving. When we forgive, we free ourselves of the negative and toxic energy that surrounds the whole issue that needs to be forgiven. Like any other negative energy, it can latch on and hang on to our bodies like a parasite, until we consciously do something to let it go. A patient asked me recently how do you forgive something that is unacceptable or unforgivable. My response was that nothing is unforgivable. Even the worst crime can be forgiven. I watched an *Oprah Winfrey Show* on forgiveness one day, and became convinced that all could be forgiven. The show focused on a woman whose daughter had been killed by a man, who is now in jail. The mother forgave the killer with all her heart. She was free. She now had peace and was able to move on with her life, instead of being emotionally tormented by the events that took her daughter from her. After seeing this, I believed that anything could be forgiven – no matter how big or small.

Forgiving Yourself

One of the hardest things to do is to forgive ourselves. However, most situations needing forgiveness include forgiving ourselves. When someone has done something to hurt us, at some level of our being, we allowed this to happen to us. For this reason, we need to forgive ourselves for letting our defences down and permitting someone to get the better of us. That being said, I am certainly not implying that we are always playing the victim, but merely vulnerable at times when others can more easily hurt us. We all allow ourselves to get into situations that are not in the best interest for our spirits. We can probably all think of one or two instances in our lives that reflect our bad choices. The fact is that we made it through, so to punish ourselves with guilt and "what ifs" for the rest of our lives is futile. When we can forgive our own mistakes, we can move forward without the negative baggage that usually tags along.

Forgiving Others

Forgiving others is one of the keys to emotional, physical and spiritual freedom. Forgiveness does not mean that you agree with or condone the behaviour of another. It merely means that you are able to let go of any negative emotional attachment to the person or situation that caused you pain. Not forgiving allows our egos to stay afloat in a world of fear. Forgiving frees our spirit into a world of positive energy. When you forgive, you are automatically propelled into a higher consciousness and state of relaxation.

Some people refuse to forgive for their entire lifetime. I find this not only sad, but also the probable cause for many illnesses. By not forgiving, the negative thought patterns associated with the events are allowed to fester in the body for years and can lead to illness.

Ask yourself if you need to forgive anyone in your life. This means your entire life. If the answer is yes, then the sooner you have the courage to do so, the better. There are many ways to forgive. I usually suggest that you forgive yourself first, and then move on to forgiving those that have hurt you. Simply setting aside some private time in which you allow any emotions to surface surrounding the event or person who you think hurt you is the first step. Next, it is helpful to consciously release any negative emotions or energy associated with the person or event. How is this done? I generally recommend that people visualize an image of the person or event, and then any negative or dark energy surrounding it floating away and changing into positive white light.

For some, it is too painful and difficult to communicate their forgiveness with another. If this is the case, I suggest to my patients that they write a letter of forgiveness addressed to the person they need to forgive. The letter doesn't ever need to be given to the person it is addressed to. Merely the action of writing the words on the paper energetically clears the negative emotions and energy from your body. In clearing these toxic emotions, the body, mind and spirit are detoxified and illness can disappear.

It sometimes helps you to forgive others, if you can put yourself into their shoes. People are not inherently cruel. They may have cruel behaviours because they developed them over time as a means to gain control over others and/or a sense of power in their lives. Unfortunately, power and control are part of what the ego longs for, not the spirit. When someone's self-esteem is low, there is often a need to feel better than others. One way of achieving this is to put others down verbally or to physically abuse them. If you can see the pain of another's spirit that would allow them to go as far as abuse, it may be easier to forgive. Someone has to be at an ultra-low point of self-worth and esteem if he or she has the ability to hurt another. I want to reiterate that I don't think we should agree that negative behaviours are okay or tolerable in our lives. I merely suggest that we forgive what holds us back from truly being free to enjoy our lives.

Another tactic that may be helpful when trying to forgive others is to not allow ourselves to be the victim in any situation. The victim role is played frequently by many who need to forgive others. Victims have the "poor me" attitude, in which they are always done wrong by. Victims rarely take any responsibility for their contributions to negative situations. Victims feel helpless and find it difficult to stand up for themselves.

CASE study

Sarah told me her sister always spoke to her in a negative way. Sarah was fed up with this behaviour and didn't know what to do. I asked her why she allowed herself to be the victim of her sister's criticism. Sarah's eyes opened wide, "I refuse to be a victim," she said. "If you had told me that in the instant when my sister was being critical of me, I would have reacted differently."

Forgiveness is unconditional. When we forgive, we cannot expect anything in return for our forgiveness. We can't expect the people who hurt us to change their behaviour in any way, or to even apologize. In all likelihood, they probably won't change anyway. We forgive to move on for ourselves.

Forgiving someone usually has an energetic component that goes along with the emotional decision to forgive. When we forgive, there is no longer the need for a tie of negative energy to the person in question. Forgiveness energetically cuts the cord of resentment and anger towards another to free both parties. What is interesting and most helpful is that, after this disconnection, there is less of a chance for negative interactions to occur again between these two people. Energy has a snowball effect. Once there is a little negative energy, it doesn't take much for more and more to accumulate quickly. But the snowball can break apart, just as easily as it formed, if enough positive energy impacts the negative. Forgiveness is positive energy. Forgiveness stops the snowball effect, and can even melt the snow or substance that allowed the problem to evolve in the first place.

Toxic Relationships

If we are to take care of our overall health, including the body, mind and spirit, we need to release toxic relationships with people who do not serve the purpose of our positive evolution.

Unfortunately, there are a lot of people out there who don't want us to be successful. They are usually closer to us than they should be. The list may include family members, friends, co-workers and acquaintances. Sometimes even parts of ourselves are our own worst enemies. We all have our little negative voice inside, which tells us we are less than we are. We need to let go of these toxic people. We tend to hang on to people in our lives that deflate us. In a way, they are like energy vampires. Part of defining our boundaries with others means severing ties with people who create toxic emotions in our lives. I am certainly not saying we should avoid relationships with everyone who pushes our buttons. I am merely suggesting that if we define our boundaries with people clearly and they are still unable to respect them, they should not be a close part of our lives.

We are not so small. We can do whatever we are destined to in this lifetime, and anyone that stands in the way of this can go somewhere else. Those who negate our greatness have no business being close to us. These "energy vampires" usually have issues around their own self-esteem, which manifest in picking on other people.

> Choose your friends wisely. Most affluent people are friends with other affluent people. You attract what you live. You are a product of your environment. If your friends now are all sick and broke, you will manifest the same. Choose to associate with people you wish to emulate and things will change!

Avoid Competition

There is absolutely no need to compete in life. When others are doing well, we should rejoice and congratulate them on their success. When others are successful, it is just an indication to ourselves that it is possible for us to do the same. Competing with others is the ego's way of gaining energy. The soul's way of gaining energy is to appreciate success in everything and everyone that touches it.

Competition places judgment on others. We judge if people are better or worse than us. Competing means there is always a winner and a loser. The beauty of living a soul-filled life is that there are no losers. We are all winners, no matter what outcomes we share. We tend to forget that we are all connected to each other via the Creator. What affects one, affects all. The more we rejoice in someone's success, the more pleasure we create for ourselves.

Live Your Dream

Dream big – very, very big. Every dream we have will be fulfilled if we want it badly enough, and put enough energy into realizing it.

I heard Deepak Chopra speak on a documentary about dharma, or your purpose in life. He said you should ask yourself: What would you be doing, if you had all the time and money in the world? This is your soul's purpose or dharma. I always tell people that if they can't do it 100 per cent now, they can at least take small steps to reach that end, every day. For example, my dream life is to write well-known books, lecture to large audiences about healing and creating affluence, and to donate large sums of money to those less fortunate in the world. So, right now, I am writing, I lecture as often as I can, and I visualize myself travelling the world to spread wealth to the underprivileged. I also believe that I am the captain of my own destiny, and all these things that I dream of will manifest some day – when they are meant to. We are on the Creator's clock, not our own.

Manifesting Dreams

The world is a haven for potential dreams. I'm sure many of us have heard the saying, "Be careful what you wish for because you might just get it." In fact, that may be the best way of describing manifestation. Whatever energy you are projecting out into the Universe, you have the potential to create. This is where we need to be careful. If we project negative energy into the Universe, we create negative situations for ourselves, slowing down our spiritual growth. If we are positive and loving, we create positive manifestations for ourselves. Unfortunately, we are not conscious about the number of negative thoughts we have about ourselves and others. If we can train our minds to be conscious of our negativity, we will have an easier time eradicating it.

In order to manifest things, we need to be aware that thoughts become words, which become actions.[44] We need to follow our intuition and start talking about our dreams. Once we are talking about it, others catch on and add their energy to the manifestation. Then we start taking actions towards manifesting our dreams. By this time, the manifestation energy is gaining more and more momentum, and accumulating more energy. Soon, it is only a matter of time before we see the physical form of our dream. In my mind, as soon as I have an intuitive breakthrough, I visualize my dream. I can see it in all its detail. The more detail you see, the better. Then I tell myself it already exists. In essence, it does. It is an energetic blueprint for the physical end product. Now all it needs is more energy to become the real thing. The energy is accumulated by talking about it and then taking action.

Creating Abundance

We create our own destiny in finances as well. We are all meant to have more abundance than we could ever use in a lifetime. Madonna was interviewed and asked why she keeps working and promoting herself, even though she has already acquired so much success. Her answer was that the more money she makes the more people she can help.

Abundance creates more abundance. The harder we work to create some abundance for ourselves and others, the better we feel. The better we feel, the more motivated we are to make more money and help more people. Money doesn't create happiness, but it sure makes life more enjoyable and less stressful when there is enough of it to go around.

Money has energy. It is an exchange in physical form of energy that is passed from one person to another. Money should be given with good intentions and positive energy. The more we give, the more we get. If we hoard all our money, there is less flow of positive energy caused by the money and, therefore, less will flow our way. I am certainly not implying that we should all spend money with reckless abandon. However, if we tend to be on the stingy side, we can gain a lot by giving. When we give, it should be for the sake of giving with our hearts, and not with the intention of getting something in return.

The more we worry about money, the less we acquire. Money and abundance have energy surrounding them. If we attach fear to abundance, it stops the flow of energy in its tracks. If we have faith about abundance, that positive energy follows the abundance and creates more of it.

Procrastination

The problem that many of us have is follow-through. We have a dream, but lack the self-confidence to follow it up and create it. The Universe has a funny way of testing our commitment to our dreams. We will encounter rejection, negativity and people telling us we are crazy on our way to achieving our goals. We need to see these instances as opportunities for growth. Every challenge we overcome gets us one step closer to actualizing our dreams.

Most of us have a tendency to procrastinate in some way. We may delay finishing our projects, mowing the lawn or de-cluttering our office. It is human nature to leave things to the last minute. We create stress for ourselves each time we have to finish something in a pinch. Stress has negative effects on our health, as I discussed earlier.

The worst time to procrastinate is when we are trying to accomplish our life goals. Each day of our lives is either a successful day or not. Each day, we have the opportunity to either add a piece of positive energy towards the production of our goals or not. At the end of each day, you could ask yourself whether it was a successful day or not. Each time you procrastinate, you are slowing down your own momentum towards actualizing your destiny. The momentum increases, the more successful days we have. The energy accumulated day to day becomes so great that it would be nearly impossible to not create our dreams.

Love Versus Fear

What I learned from Marianne Williamson, an authority in living a spiritually fulfilled life, was that every thought, word and action comes from a place of either love or fear. We are a fear-driven society and our lesson is to live with more love in this lifetime. When we choose loving thoughts and actions, life runs more smoothly. If we want to be truly happy and healthy, we need to live in love—and not in fear.

Fear runs the life of so many. We fear the unknown. We fear things that we feel we can't control. We fear life. Fear pollutes our bodies, minds and spirits. Fear holds us back from accomplishing our goals in life, and living to our full potential. Fear is like a tranquilizer that puts our bodies in a state of sedation. When we are fearful, we are less able to take the steps necessary to propel us forward along our paths. Why do we fear so much? We have a general lack of faith in the Universe, in God, in ourselves.

How do we become less fearful and move towards love? The simplest way is to train ourselves to be less negative. Every negative thought, word or action comes from a place of fear and not love. Negative thoughts roll through the minds of so many of us, without our even being conscious of it. Start to pay attention to the number of negative thoughts you have in a day. You will be surprised. I know I was when I first tuned into my negative thinking patterns. What is even more fun is to pick up on how many negative thoughts or words the people around you express, after you have mastered your own negative thought analysis.

The next part of the exercise is to instantly turn a negative thought into a positive one. I always use this example with my patients: Let's say that the weather outside is rainy, dark and miserable. A positive spin on the situation is that the rain is a good thing because it keeps the beautiful grass green and the trees alive. Even visualizing the positive outlook makes you feel better and more positive in the moment. This is love and not fear. Love makes you feel good. Love keeps you healthy. Love attracts one of its physical counterparts – MONEY!

CHAPTER 12 | A SOUL-FULL LIFE

Living a Soul-Full Life

Living a soul-full life means living with vigour, enthusiasm and a joie de vivre. We are complex beings, with a need to nurture our bodies, minds and spirits. I think many of us forget the spiritual aspect of ourselves. Many of us probably don't even know what it is. If we start to listen to our inner voice, or intuition, we can be guided through life in a less difficult and painful way than how we would usually choose on our own. We are meant to enjoy the ride of life and really live it, rather than just to exist and go through the motions. Every day is a good day. Some days may have challenges, but when we choose to see the bigger picture – why we are here, and what we are meant to do in this lifetime – the challenges become the lessons that teach us how to be better individuals.

Your Soul's Purpose

Everyone was put on this earth to accomplish a certain task. We all have a unique talent and/or knowledge of specific things to allow us to complete this task. God gave some people a beautiful voice to share with the world and make us happier. Could you imagine if Celine Dion had not followed her soul's purpose and we never heard her voice? We all have something very special to offer the world. If more of us tapped into our natural gifts – no matter how intellectually ridiculous they might seem – the world would be filled with so many more wonderful things. A good example of this is the story of a very famous purple dinosaur we all know. The idea of Barney was derided by a boardroom of adults, who thought a giant, purple dinosaur would not be popular. When Barney was presented to a group of children, of course, they loved it, and the rest is history. Barney is now a multimillion-dollar industry.

So how do you determine your soul's purpose? Ask yourself what makes you truly happy If you try to do things every day that make your soul happy, you will eventually attract everything you need to fulfil your destiny. Soul-level actions, which you take every second of every day, help to lead you to where you are meant to go. For most people, it is not a big break that gets them to where they need to be in life, but the little baby steps that led up to the opportunities of their lifetime. On a daily basis, we can ask ourselves if we feel we have accomplished something towards our spiritual goals in life, with joy. If the answer is yes, then we are well on our way to ultimate fulfilment and joy.

Childhood interests that separated us from everyone else may be hints towards our soul's purpose in life. If you ask most professional athletes when they knew they would be successful at their chosen sport, they usually answer that, in their early childhood, they had an unexplained passion for that activity.

Tapping Into Your Intuition

Our intuition can guide us to the answers we need in terms of our soul's purpose. The definition of intuition is, "the immediate knowing of something, without the conscious use of reasoning."[45] Intuition is inherent. We are all born with intuition. As children, we were probably more intuitive than we are now as adults. Young children have not yet been socialized to believe that only what can be seen, heard and felt in the physical form exists. As they age, they are told that their imaginary friends are just that, imaginary. In reality, children are quite aware of what is going on in their surroundings. Parents need to be aware that when a child is frightened by "the boogeyman," or a monster under the bed or in the closet, there may actually be some negative energy lurking exactly where they say it is. The key is to acknowledge the energy and avoid fearing it in any way.

My son amazed me at the age of three when he told me that, "Daddy's cell phone is broken," when Daddy was overseas. When I called my husband two minutes later, and he told me his cell phone wasn't working properly, I was amazed, but not really.

Practice makes perfect. The same is true for intuition. The more we use our intuitive mind, the sharper it becomes. The most challenging thing about intuition is trusting and following the hunches we get. It is one thing to have a feeling about something or someone, but entirely different to use this information for our own good. How many times have you said to yourself, "I should have followed my instincts"? Even when the intuitive messages we receive seem off the wall and crazy, we need to have more confidence in following them. It is usually the most obscure intuitions that bring us the best results, because they are far beyond what we would imagine for ourselves.

CASE study

Anita, a thirty-three-year-old woman, was shy in telling me that her ability to pick up on other's energy or intentions was very acute. She thought her ability to tune into energy beyond the physical had negative consequences. She told me that she once walked into a room and knew that an individual present had negative energy and was judging her, without this person even saying a word. Anita thought that it was a bad thing to be able to intuitively know this. I assured her that intuition is never "bad," and is only there to protect us. She probably picked up on this person's energy so that she would know to avoid interactions with him or her.

It's the Journey That Counts

Don't get caught up in outcomes. Expectations lead to disappointments. What has really helped me in my journey thus far is a sense that God or the Universe has so much more planned for me than I can even imagine. What is important is to enjoy the journey, every day, and the baby steps that need to be taken to reach our destinies. Life is about the journey and the lessons we learn along the way. If we learn the lessons effectively, we move on to the next step. It is just like grade school. The board of education sets out certain curricula for each grade. The students learn the work, step by step. When they have effectively learned the lessons, they move on to the next grade, and so on. The same is true for life lessons. The Universe presents us with certain lessons to learn, such as how to be more generous, or kind, or less judgmental of others. If we learn the lesson, our life moves on and we face our next lesson. If, however, we don't learn the lesson, the Universe presents similar situations until we get it. This is why so many of us stay stuck in the same grade of life for a very long time. We need to ask ourselves, "Okay, what am I supposed to learn from this situation in order to move on and be a better person?"

Finding Happiness

To be truly happy, one may have to detoxify obstacles to happiness. Happiness is inherent. We are here to be happy. Unfortunately, many of us live in the delusional world of suffering, heartache and misery. These are just an illusion. These obstacles keep us stuck in this negative pattern:

- Inability to let go of the past
- Guilt
- Fear
- Conditions on love
- Inability to forgive
- Unstable relationships
- Illness

If we do not address these obstacles to happiness, we may never get there. Being happy means being free from negative thoughts or fears. Only when we are truly happy can we move forward towards our soul's destiny.

Happiness can be a reality for everyone, although it is the exception instead of the norm. Some of us don't even know or remember what happiness is. Happy people are healthy. Unfortunately, I don't meet too many people that are truly happy in my business. The majority of patients who come to see me are in some way sick. I try to remind everyone that we are here to enjoy ourselves, not to suffer.

We can all find something to do that makes us happy. Whether it is taking a walk on a forest trail, going out to a movie or dancing the night away, we all have small things that make us happy. It is important to incorporate these things into our busy schedules for our health. I ask many of my patients if they can remember a time when they were truly content. Most of them have an instant memory of a time in their lives when everything was going great. I then explain that if they can emulate parts of what they were doing at that time now, they may find some happiness again.

CASE study

Sandy, a twenty-seven-year-old man, came to see me for his depression, fatigue, obesity and headaches. He explained to me that his life was now in complete chaos. He had a domineering mother who put him down his whole life. I asked him if he could remember a time when he felt happy. He said he felt on top of the world when he was running his own business, living in his own place and doing his own thing. He used to do interior design. His life now was the total opposite. He was working with his mother in the same office where his mother could control him all day long. Sandy was in tears and realized he needed to somehow regain his independence to be happy again. His soul's purpose was in the arts, being creative and working for others on his own terms. When he realized this, he was more motivated to make changes for himself to push him towards his goals in life. He later opened his own interior design company and became very successful in a short amount of time.

Being True to Your Feelings

I don't know how many times I have asked friends or acquaintances how they are doing and they say, "I'm fine," and I know they are not. It doesn't take a genius to know when someone close to you is not at his or her best. For some reason, we don't like to share our hardships with others. In fact, our friends may be the best help, if we had the courage to share our true feelings. There are some who go to the opposite extreme and don't shut up about their daily woes. This again is not ideal, because talking about negativity all the time only attracts more to you. So, if someone asks you how you are doing, tell them the truth.

Grace

Being grateful for all we have is paramount. When we can acknowledge and give thanks for all we have been given, we can lead a fulfilled life. If we have an outlook that only sees lack, we will never achieve or have enough.

I wrote the following poem and read it over the radio shortly after I graduated from naturopathic college. I had people calling the radio station to get a copy of it because it was so powerful to them. In my naivety, I didn't realize that such simple words, which I conjured up one night when I was bored, would have such an impact.

This poem hangs on the wall in my dad's house and is a reminder to me, whenever I read it, that I need to be grateful for everything I am, I have and will have in the future.

Dear God, Creator and Universal Energy,
I thank you for who I am, what I do and where I am going;
I thank you for showing yourself to me, day in, day out.
I thank you for the sun in the sky that illuminates
my world and my heart.
I thank you for my parents, my siblings, my children.
I thank you for my wisdom, my beauty and my ability
to be your messenger.
I thank you for the lessons I have learned,
and will continue to learn.
I thank you for your forgiveness and unconditional love.
I thank you for the light I am able to see in my heart — your light.
I only hope I can continue to be what you intended for me,
which is a piece of you, a piece of perfection.
Thank you, thank you, thank you

To obtain a free, printable copy of this poem,
go to www.healthymillionairebook.com.

Take Responsibility for Your Health

It is far too easy for some people to blame others for their health problems, when we cause most of our ailments all on our own. Negative thinking is the biggest culprit, which leads to ill health over time. I know from experience that the happiest and most fulfilled people in life have the fewest ailments or health concerns. People who are miserable are more likely to be sick for a large part of their lives. You attract to you what you put out into the Universe. If your thoughts are positive and you can see minor changes in your body as signals to improve your mental, spiritual or physical health, then serious illness will be less likely to be apart of your existence. If, however, you take every ache or pain in your body as a signal of impending disease or misery, or you do not make the necessary positive changes in your mind, body and spirit, you are more likely to create serious illness in your system.

Taking responsibility for our health requires that we look more deeply into why we may be sick. Aches and pains, repetitive colds and flus, headaches and all other symptoms are all indications that something is out of balance in our lives. Most of us would rather take a Tylenol and be done with it. Unfortunately, this is not real healing. Sure our symptoms will clear up, but the underlying cause still remains. For instance, a chronic lack of sleep may be the real culprit that causes our immune system to be weak, which, in turn, causes chronic colds. Another example may be a nagging mother-in-law that causes headaches. When we look more deeply, we can often find the root cause of our ailments — in line with the principles of naturopathic medicine.

In the example of a nagging mother-in-law, boss or co-worker, it is our responsibility to change our attitude or involvement with those who push our buttons. Taking responsibility for our health means looking at why this person is in our life, and why do we let them bother us so much? Only if we change our behaviour is there any chance for real healing.

CHAPTER 13 | CHAKRAS

Chakras

Chakra is a Sanskrit word meaning wheel or vortex. The chakras are energy centres located in seven different places on the body. They are found along the midline of the body, and each has a front and back component. The chakras have their own spiritual, mental and physical connections to the body. They function as pumps or valves to release or accumulate energy. If the chakras are not functioning properly, illness can arise in the corresponding part of the body that the chakra is near.

Balancing the Chakras

Each chakra has its own energy field at a certain frequency and vibration. What is important is that a balance is achieved throughout the chakras. Many have been told that their "chakras are out of balance." What this means is that the energy in some is higher or lower than in the rest. When we have chronic deficiencies or excesses of energy in certain chakras, it is reflected in our day-to-day life through the circumstances we find ourselves in, and the way our physical body works.

CASE study

I had a patient who had severe financial troubles most of his life. He also developed prostatitis from time to time, which is an infection of the prostate gland. When I scanned his chakras, I noticed an abundance of energy in his second chakra – the chakra of relationships with others, money and sex. He also alluded to long-term troubles in his relationships with women. After I had balanced out this extra energy in the second chakra with energy healing and craniosacral therapy, he reported that his finances were stabilizing, his prostatitis disappeared, and his ability to maintain healthy relationships had improved. Now, whether his chakra was out of balance first, or his troubles relating to the second chakra caused it to be overactive is anyone's guess. What is important is that finding a balance throughout all his chakras was necessary for his well-being – both emotional and physical.

Chart of the Chakras

CHAKRA	LOCATION	COLOUR	SPIRITUAL	MENTAL	PHYSICAL
1	Base of spine, tailbone	Red	Tribal energy, one's grounding to Earth	Relationship with tribe, relationship with Mother Earth	Tailbone, legs, knees, ankles, feet and toes
2	Sacrum, pelvis	Orange	Power of reproduction	Relationship with others, sex, money	Pelvic or sexual organs
3	Solar plexus	Yellow	Love of self, ego	Relationship with self	Liver, kidneys, spleen, small and large intestines
4	Heart	Green	Love of all things	Love	Heart, ribs
5	Throat	Blue	Will power	Ability to express self	Thyroid, neck
6	Third eye	Indigo	Intuition	Following inner guidance with confidence	Eyes, ears, sinuses
7	Top of head	Violet	Connection with the Universe	Having faith	Head

The First Chakra

The first chakra is the foundation of the physical body. It includes the feet, legs and tailbone. The energy of the first chakra grounds a person and allows them to feel safe and secure in their environment. First chakra energy governs the immune system. The psycho-spiritual links of the first chakra involve tribal energy. Feeling connectedness to one's tribe or family surroundings develops very early in life. This can be linked to the immune system, which is not fully developed until the age of seven. If you think of a child, most of his or her life revolves around the family until he or she reaches seven or eight, when the child begins to become more independent. As the immune system matures, so does the strength of the child's independence.

People who have weak immune systems may have blocks in their first chakra energy. Mike developed mononucleosis during his first year at university. It was the first time he had moved away from home and was living in residence. Mike was not grounded or feeling safe and secure in his new environment at school. This was a challenge to the energy in his first chakra, making him more susceptible to picking up viruses, because his immune system was somewhat suppressed.

Trust is an issue of the first chakra. Trust develops early in life with when we emerge into the world as helpless infants. If any trust is lost during our upbringing, we may manifest symptoms associated with the first chakra.

To strengthen the first chakra, it is important to be grounded. You can try the following exercise to become grounded and strengthen your immune system.

Grounding exercise for the first chakra

Sit or lie down comfortably on your back. Imagine energy coming in through the top of your head and down the midline of your body, to your tailbone, down your legs and out through the bottom of your feet. Then picture the energy going through the ground and connecting with the centre of the earth. At some point, you may feel a shift in your energy. This is when you are grounded and connected to the earth.

Two postures that strengthen the first chakra are mountain pose and tree pose (see below).

Tadasana

(Mountain pose)

Stand with your feet hip-width apart, the weight distributed evenly in both feet. Relax the shoulders down and pull in the belly. Look straight ahead. Lengthen the spine by imagining a pulling action down your legs, connecting you to the centre of the earth. Use the breath to lengthen towards the sky, from the torso up. Breathe deeply and feel your strength.

This posture is the starting point of all the standing postures. It entails much more than it appears. It helps to root and strengthen the first chakra.

Vrksasana

(Tree pose)

Start in mountain pose with feet hip-width apart. Bend one leg and place the heel of that foot on the inside of the other leg, as high up as comfortable so you can still keep your balance. Use your hand to stabilize your bent leg as necessary. Exhale and root your energy into the floor. Bring your arms above your head and breathe. Focus your vision on one point to help to keep your balance. Release the bent leg back to the floor and the arms by your sides.
Repeat on the other leg.[46]

The Second Chakra

The second chakra includes the reproductive organs, lower back, sacrum, kidneys, bladder, urinary tract and the lower part of the intestinal tract. The second chakra deals with relationship issues with other people. It is the sex chakra, the money centre and the area that controls our drive in life to achieve our goals. If the second chakra is blocked, it can lead to reproductive difficulties, kidney problems and lower back pain, to name a few. At an emotional level, if the second chakra lacks energy, one may have difficulty forming healthy relationships with others. Some people with an issue in the second chakra also find it difficult to pursue their dreams or aspirations in life, because they lack the assertiveness and drive that come from the second chakra.

CASE study

Doreen came to see me for some energetic healing. She didn't have any specific complaints or ailments at the time. She just wanted to experience a shift in her energy fields. I tuned into her second chakra right at the beginning of the session. I was able to detect that the energy here was very deficient, as compared with her other chakras. I had a sense that there had been some trauma to this area in her past. I allowed new, positive energy to flow through this chakra, and then balanced the energy with the other chakras. When we finished our session, Doreen said that she had a secret abortion when she was twenty-one. She didn't tell anyone, including her family and her friends. Since that time, she never ovulated again and her menstrual cycles were abnormal. She admitted to a strong emotional tie to this event that she still hadn't let go of. The next time I saw Doreen, a few months later, she was happy to report that she was ovulating again and felt she had fully dealt with the emotional trauma of the abortion.

This was a great example of how an emotionally and physically traumatic event had an effect on the functioning of a chakra's energy. When the energy was cleared, as well as letting go of the emotional link to the event that caused the blockage, normal function was restored in the reproductive system.

Clearing exercise for the second chakra

Stand with feet hip-width apart and knees slightly bent. Rock the pelvis forward and back repeatedly. Imagine you have a string with a pencil on it tied around your waist and hanging down to the ground. The aim is to draw a perpendicular line between your legs with the pencil, by only moving your pelvis. This exercise helps to free the energy in the second chakra and keeps the sacrum mobile.

The Third Chakra

The third chakra is at the level of the solar plexus, or upper abdomen. It is the chakra of self-esteem. This chakra deals with the feelings that we have about ourselves. It includes the stomach, intestines, spleen, liver, gallbladder and nervous system. The spiritual theme of the third chakra revolves around loving ourselves. People also relate this chakra to intuition and following your "gut instinct."

I commonly see an energetic hole in the third chakra that usually corresponds to low self-esteem. Many of my patients have not been consciously aware that they had low self-esteem until I started to talk to them about it. They just felt as if everyone felt this way about themselves.

Exercise for strengthening the third chakra

Visualize pure, white light entering the area from just below the rib cage to just below the belly button. With this energy, repeat the affirmation, "I love myself. I am perfect the way I am. I am whole and complete. I am the perfect me."

The Fourth Chakra

The heart chakra is located in the centre of the chest, in line with the breasts. It is the master chakra, responsible for allowing loving energy into the body and then out again. The heart centre is the chakra in the centre of all the other chakras, with three above and three below. If the heart chakra becomes blocked, the entire system suffers because a lack of vital energy enters the body. The worst-case outcome of a closed heart chakra is a heart attack. The physical heart stops beating, in response to emotional stress or a blockage in blood flow to the heart.

The blocked blood flow usually exists long before the heart attack, because the person has restricted the positive flow of energy through the heart chakra.

The front of the heart chakra deals with our loving relationships with others. If the front of this chakra is open, we have an easier time with love, relationships and intimacy. If it is closed, we may not be as open to engaging in loving relationships with others.

The back of the heart chakra has to do with one's will, and trust of others. If the back portion of the heart chakra is closed, one may have a difficult time standing up for oneself.

Exercise to open the fourth chakra
One of the best yoga postures for opening the heart chakra is cobra.

Bhujangasana
Cobra
Lie on your stomach. With hands at your sides, at the level just ahead of the shoulders, slowly push yourself up to rest on your forearms. Your neck should remain extended and long. Use the breath to open the rib cage and expand the chest. Exhale and slowly lower yourself down to the ground.

This is not recommended for those with weak lower backs.
Cobra opens the chest and heart chakra.[47]

The Fifth Chakra

The fifth chakra is the throat chakra. It includes the throat, thyroid gland, vocal cords and the uppermost part of the lungs. This chakra deals with expression, the ability to express our truths and our will. If one is blocked in this area, they may have problems with sore throats, thyroid gland imbalances, voice abnormalities or chronic upper respiratory tract infections. It is very important for us to be able to express our true feelings as they relate to our consciousness. If we have difficulty in doing so, we may become blocked in the fifth chakra.

A very good example of a blocked fifth chakra is hypothyroidism. This is a condition, common in women, that is characterized by low body temperature, weight gain, dry skin, falling hair, constipation, fatigue and moodiness. It is a result of the thyroid gland in the neck, not functioning adequately to produce the necessary thyroid hormones that help to regulate metabolism. Usually, a medical doctor would prescribe thyroxine, the deficient hormone. The patient will definitely feel better on this medication, but, after a time, the gland will begin to rely on the drug, and may become lazy and stop functioning on its own. At this time, a higher dose of the drug may need to be given.

On the other hand, when the thyroid gland is healed at the root cause of its imbalance, there is potentially a cure for the condition. A person who has difficulty expressing him or herself may develop hypothyroidism after a while and a block in the fifth chakra.

The energy blockage can be healed in a variety of ways. I use craniosacral therapy, but other practitioners may use reiki, therapeutic touch, reflexology or any other energy healing technique. Freeing the energy in this area, coupled with an improvement in self-expression, the patient can potentially alleviate the hypothyroidism completely.

Exercise for opening the fifth chakra

The best exercise for freeing the fifth chakra is using our voice. In yoga, a great posture for increasing energy and blood flow to the throat and thyroid gland is bridge pose (see below).

Setu bandha sarvangasana

(Bridge pose)

Lie on your back with knees bent. Start with feet hip-width apart. Place your arms at your sides. Move your feet as close to your sitting bones as possible. Inhale and lift your buttocks off the ground, so you are balancing on your feet and shoulders. Stay in this position for a few breaths. As you inhale, scoop your abdomen in towards your spine. Exhaling, slowly lower yourself back to the ground and stretch your legs to rest in corpse pose.

You may want to hug your knees into your chest as a counter pose, to release any tension in your back after doing the bridge.

The Sixth Chakra

The sixth chakra is the third-eye chakra. The third eye, located between the actual eyes, is the seat of intuitive vision and the ability to see non-physical energies. The sixth chakra also includes the sinuses and the ears. On a mental level, this chakra allows the mind to trust, and then follow the intuitive messages we receive. When this chakra is open, we see more truths and what we are meant to see for our higher purpose. When this chakra is closed, we are not quite in tune with the laws of the Universe and the path that we should probably be on.

Healers are a good example of people whose sixth chakra is usually open. They use their intuition and third eye to help others to see what ails them.

Exercise to open the sixth chakra

Visualize a large eye between your two eyes. With your eyes closed, visualize positive energy or white light entering the area of the third eye. Now envision your third eye opening up, as if the eyelid is slowly lifting to uncover it.

One yoga posture that strengthens the third eye is child's pose. The third eye connects with the ground as the entire body rests. Child's pose is a wonderful way to relax after doing backbends or strenuous postures.

Pranatasana

(Child's pose)

Sit on your heels. Bend forward and let your arms rest either in front of you on the floor, or at your sides with your palms faced up. Place your head on the floor, letting your forehead rest on the floor. Exhale, and let your spine lengthen with your hips dropping towards the heels. Relax your head, neck and shoulders.

The Seventh Chakra

The crown, or seventh chakra is located on the crown of the head. It is the highest energy centre, where Universal Energy enters our body. On a mental level, it deals with the acceptance of the existence of the higher power of the Universe, and allows it to enter our lives.

I have commonly found this chakra to be closed in people who suffer from chronic headaches, especially when the headache is located at the top of the head. I have seen a pattern in people who tend to be stubborn, in that their seventh chakra is often closed. Sceptics also often have a closed seventh chakra, as they do not allow the Universal energy to enter their systems in the first place.

Exercise to open the seventh chakra

To open the seventh chakra, visualize energy entering the top of the head and travelling down the rest of the chakras to the feet and connecting with the centre of the Earth. In Chinese medicine, there is an acupuncture point in the centre of the top of the head called Governing Vessel 20. Find it by connecting a line between the tops of each ear in one direction, and a line drawn from the tip of the nose in the other direction. You can tap this point to increase your brain power and alertness, but also to stimulate the seventh chakra.

More Chakras

Some believe that there are more than the seven standard chakras. I believe this is probably true. However, to keep things simple, I chose to focus on the first seven.

CHAPTER 14 | NATUROPATHIC REMEDIES FOR DETOXIFYING THE SPIRIT

Thankfully, naturopathic medicine offers modalities and remedies that address the aspect of spirit, which is often overlooked. A healthy spirit usually transfers into a healthy mind and body. Spiritual health may be the missing link in modern medicine, and certainly deserves more attention as we evolve as human beings in a toxic world.

Acupuncture

Acupuncture has the ability to cleanse and calm the spirit. One point in particular, called Shen Men, calms the spirit and the chi of the entire body. It is called the "Spirit Gate" or "God's Door." There is a Shen Men ear acupuncture point, as well as a heart meridian point located on the inner wrist crease. The points can either be needled by a qualified practitioner, or you can use acupressure by pressing the point or by using small clockwise circular pressure at the points.

The point Heart 7 is located on the palmar side of the wrist crease in the depression at the proximal border of the pisiform bone. It is on the large wrist crease, palm facing upwards on the side of the pinky finger, just inside the tendon in the small depression.

Classical Homeopathy

Homeopathy can be very helpful for detoxification of the body, mind and spirit. Homeopathic remedies are very dilute substances derived from a plant, animal or mineral source. They work according to the law of similars, in which the symptoms caused by a substance in an undiluted form will be alleviated when the sick individual is given the substance in homeopathic dilutions. Homeopathic doctors ask a lot of questions. The answers to these questions help the doctor to determine a theme that coincides with the essence of the remedy.

CASE study

Nora, a twenty-two-year-old woman, was a naturopathic student in her first year at naturopathic college. Her chief complaint was depression, since her mother died three years earlier. She took the homeopathic remedy Natrum Mur. The first week after taking the remedy, she had dreams about her mother and cried every day. She was finally grieving her mother's death. The homeopathic remedy was the impetus to change Nora's mental/emotional status for the better. After that week of tears, she started to feel much better, with more energy from day to day, and eventually the depression lifted and never returned.

Bodywork

Naturopathic bodywork is very similar to massage therapy. Naturopathic doctors are trained in the technique of Swedish massage. Bodywork can be extremely detoxifying, because you are moving the lymph around that is located just under the skin's surface. I usually warn my patients that they may feel tired after a massage, or even get sick with a cold, because the toxins have been mobilized to be cleared by the body. I have even had the experience of a headache after a massage from the release of toxins into the blood. These are examples of a healing crisis.

When you allow yourself to fully surrender and relax during a massage, it may be easier for you to let go of emotional and spiritual issues that influence your life. A good friend of mine is a massage therapist and tells me she can't believe how much people open up to her during a massage. They divulge their innermost secrets and fears, because they feel safe and taken care of during a massage.

Spiritual Healing

One day in August 2006, I went to listen to a pastor from Africa speak. I came home from the church thinking the whole point of my book was useless, because, according to his experience, all you have to do is to pray to God for healing, and it shall be done. I believe this. So, why do we even need remedies, herbs and other people to help us through our ailments, if all we need is God? I guess the more faith we have, the less we need these other means to help us heal.

I believe all natural remedies are small bits from God or a higher power. They give us something tangible to believe in and, thus, help us to eradicate disease. God knows that most of us believe we need to physically take things to help us get well. In fact, we only need our belief in Him or a higher power. Spiritual healing uses this belief. There are many light-workers, healers and pastors who help others to heal at a spiritual and energetic level, which in turn heals the physical body. There are few diseases or ailments that cannot be healed if you believe. If your mind believes you can be healed, you can be healed. Some believe in their minds that they can only be healed if, for example, their sick organ is surgically removed, and, for them, this is the only way for them to get better. I never argue with a patient who intuitively knows what will work and what won't work for their healing. We are all our own best doctors, when our intuition is finely tuned and accurate.

We may pose the question: Why are some people born with disabilities, genetic diseases and cancers that occur early in life? I believe that, in these cases, there is a gift to be learned for that individual, and the caregivers in this lifetime. For those who believe in past lives and the afterlife, there may be karmic reasons why we experience certain ailments in this lifetime. Karma is timeless and continues into infinity. What you sow, you reap – including from times before, and continuing well after the present moment.

The same pastor told us about an event that had happened during one of his sermons. He said he asked the congregation to place a hand on whatever part of their body was sick. One woman placed her hand on her abdomen because she had a uterine fibroid. He then said wherever they needed to be healed, would be – by the Creator in that instant. Years later, the pastor met this woman again and she carried a jar containing her fibroid. She told him that after his sermon years ago, the Creator allowed that fibroid to fall from her body. There are countless other stories such as this.

Prayer/Meditation

I cannot extol the virtues of meditation and prayer enough. Meditation is easy to learn and practise. It does not need to be any complex set of postures or breathing patterns as many believe. You can meditate anywhere – on the bus, in the shower, or even when exercising. Meditation means to take your mind away from its usual chatter and let it rest for a while. Meditation allows the nervous system to enter the parasympathetic or relaxed state. This is the state needed for detoxification, as well as for healing.

Transcendental meditation (TM) is one of the most widely used and studied types of meditation. TM participants are taught to meditate by repeating a word, sound or phrase, called a mantra, over and over again for twenty minutes. TM is usually practised before breakfast and dinner, when you are less likely to fall asleep. When outside thoughts enter your head, you can quickly disregard them by repeating your mantra. The Sanskrit word "Om" is commonly used by TM practitioners, because it has a soothing sound, especially when repeated.[48]

Prayer usually has intent. We pray for more money, a better job, to be safe and protected, and so on. Prayer to be physically and emotionally well can also have very positive effects on the body. The use of prayer for healing has been studied all around the world.

Craniosacral Therapy

Craniosacral therapy is a gentle, hands-on healing technique that treats the cranium (head) and the sacrum (the bone just above the tailbone), as well as all other parts of the body. Craniosacral therapy can be used to discover blockages in energy in a patient's body, whether from a physical, emotional or spiritual cause. Energy blockages can lead to chronic aches and pains, as well as a number of health concerns if not released. Craniosacral therapy has been helpful for the following conditions:

- Headaches
- Migraines
- Earaches
- Sinusitis
- Back pain
- Joint pain
- Sports injuries
- Arthritis
- Muscle tension
- Attention Deficit Disorder (ADD), Attention Deficit Hyperactivity Disorder (ADHD)
- Birth trauma

- Learning disabilities
- Menstrual cramps or problems
- Temporomandibular Joint (TMJ) dysfunction
- Carpal tunnel syndrome

Craniosacral therapy is an energetic healing technique that goes beyond physical healing. In many of my treatments, patients have undergone deep spiritual changes in their lives. The shifts that happen in the craniosacral system allow you to open up areas of deeper emotional and spiritual issues, of which you may not have been conscious.

I have found craniosacral therapy to be very helpful in healing traumas after an accident, particularly motor vehicle accidents. I always ask my patients if they saw the accident coming before impact. Nine times out of ten, they did see their impending crash. I have found that most of these accident victims had a sense of true fear just before impact. The fear of anticipation – from the time of the accident – stays stuck in the body, mind and spirit if it is not released. One of the few ways of releasing this tissue memory is through craniosacral therapy.

A patient, Denise, described the last few seconds before her accident as a slow-motion movie, in which she knew how to brace herself to avoid the worst possible outcome. However, Denise had suffered headaches every day of her life since the accident, which was eleven years before. She also felt stuck, and her life had not progressed spiritually since the accident. After ten minutes of craniosacral, her headache disappeared and she felt different at a deeper level of her being. The therapy reversed the memory of the accident, so she could now progress in her life as she was meant to – on physical, emotional and spiritual levels.

Somatoemotional Release

Somatoemotional Release (SER) is the identification and release of emotions or trauma stored in the tissue and cells of our bodies. Using gentle touch, imagery and dialogue, the patient and practitioner can connect with these memory cells, allowing the body an opportunity to release old patterns. SER evolved from the foundations of craniosacral therapy. Dr. John Upledger, D.O., O.M.M. has worked diligently over the past thirty years to develop the techniques taught to craniosacral therapy/somatoemotional release (CST/SER) practitioners.

All cells have tissue memory. It is like a tape recording of everything that has happened to the cell on the mental, physical and spiritual level. As the body releases stress and tension, the cellular memory held within related organs, glands, tissues, muscle and fascia begins to awaken and present itself. The patient will either have recall of these memories during the SER process, or within the twenty-four to forty-eight hours following. As suppressed emotions move out of the body, patients will experience a more relaxed and lighter feeling. If left untreated, certain emotions or trauma can evolve into anger, fear, destructive behaviour or chronic illness. Unresolved emotions are toxic, and act as such on an unsuspecting person. Through the SER process, we can gain a clearer vision of our body/mind/spirit integration, and enjoy a happier, healthier and more balanced lifestyle.

Young children and animals seem to adapt to this process more quickly than adults, as they innately know how to release what doesn't feel good to them. The adult mind holds reasoning powers, which can stand in the way of healing.

Conclusion

In conclusion, I can only hope I have conveyed this information in a way that influences people in a positive way. Whether you are a successful millionaire, or aspire to become one, it is vitally important that you achieve and maintain good health. Remember: You cannot effectively enjoy the wealth you have created if you are ill. We can all improve our toxic exposure in some way to lessen the burden on our already overwhelmed bodies, minds and spirits.

To talk about detoxification without including mental/emotional and spiritual health, to me, is pointless. We are complex creatures who function at many levels from day to day. Even if we are not aware of the higher centres of consciousness above the physical body, they still exist and need to be in a healthy balanced state – just as much as the body we can feel, touch and see.

To keep it simple: Eat well, exercise, be happy and follow your dreams! Know that you create your destiny, be it financially or in terms of your health. You have the right to create and then enjoy all that this wonderful world has to offer, as a **HEALTHY MILLIONAIRE!!!**

ABOUT THE **AUTHOR**

JANINE BOWRING

Dr. Janine Bowring, ND has been practising energetic healing since 1994, and naturopathic medicine since 1998, when she graduated from the Canadian College of Naturopathic Medicine in Toronto. Dr. Bowring, ND works at Woodbridge Naturopathic Clinic, which she founded in 2005, and is the formulator for VitaTree™ Nutritionals. Raised in St. Catharines, Ontario, she now lives with her husband and three children in the Greater Toronto Area. She also founded The Janine Bowring Foundation, a charity that supports families in impoverished countries. Part of the proceeds of this book will go to this foundation.
www.healthymillionairebook.com

About The Janine Bowring Foundation

The Healthy Millionaire™ is committed to bridging the gap between impoverished children and their families. Proceeds of The Healthy Millionaire™ and its subsidiaries are donated to The Janine Bowring Foundation (JBF). Most citizens of developing nations lack the basic essentials of life, namely food, water and shelter. The JBF is committed to creating healthy lifestyles for the less fortunate by providing food, clean water, and educational materials.

The JBF will start its programs in more than ten developing countries. Long-term community programs will benefit more than one million children and impact the lives of five million more people. The JBF is not affiliated with any religious, political, or government sectors.
www.jbfcanada.org

Appendix 1

VITAMIN / MINERAL	GOOD FOOD SOURCES	TOXICITY / CONTRAINDICATIONS	DETOXIFICATION PATHWAYS IT SUPPORTS	SYMPTOMS OF DEFICIENCY
Vitamin A	Retinol (preformed vitamin A): liver, fish oil, egg yolk, whole milk, butter, cream Beta-carotene: seaweed, spinach, asparagus, parsley, lettuce, carrots, sweet potato, pumpkin, red cabbage, apricot, peach, mango, cherry, watermelon	Fat-soluble vitamin, too much preformed vitamin A can lead to slight brain swelling and headaches Diabetics and hypothyroid patients may have difficulty converting beta-carotene into vitamin A	Helps white blood cells to eradicate toxins	Dry bumpy skin on backs of arms/legs, night blindness, cancer, low immunity, rapid aging of skin, acne, boils, periodontal disease, kidney stones
Vitamin D	Fish liver oil, salmon, mackerel, sardine, herring, egg yolk, butter, liver, fortified milk, mushroom	Overdose of vitamin D causes headaches, nausea and vomiting, diarrhea and calcification in kidneys, lungs and ears Corticosteroids such as prednisone decrease vitamin D in the body		Fractures, osteoporosis, tooth decay, gum problems
Vitamin E	Wheat germ oil, sunflower seed, almond, pecan, hazelnut, sweet potato, avocado, mango, spinach, soya bean	Interacts with warfarin and coumarin, increasing anti-clotting effects Diabetics with retinal bleeding use with caution Not recommended before surgery Vitamin E is inactivated by iron	Anti-oxidant effect that quenches free radicals Protects fatty acids from oxidation	Dry skin Prevention of aging Menstrual pain Muscle cramps Cataracts Easy bruising Sickle cell anemia Fibrocystic breasts Cancer

VITAMIN / MINERAL	GOOD FOOD SOURCES	TOXICITY / CONTRAINDICATIONS	DETOXIFICATION PATHWAYS IT SUPPORTS	SYMPTOMS OF DEFICIENCY
Vitamin C	Acerola cherry, camu camu berry, rose hip, orange juice, red chilli pepper, watermelon, papaya, cantaloupe, strawberry, kiwi, Brussel sprouts, cauliflower, broccoli, mango	Too much vitamin C causes diarrhea Gout, vitamin C increases excretion of uric acid Caution with kidney stones Synthetic vitamin C (ascorbic acid) is derived from corn, so those with corn allergies should avoid this form	Detoxifies drugs such as cortisone, aspirin and insulin Anti-oxidant that works with vitamin E and glutathione Detoxifies heavy metals: arsenic, lead and mercury	Low immunity, allergies, colds and flus, chronic stress, wound healing, cervical dysplasia, cancer, easy bruising, heavy metal toxicity, schizophrenia, cataracts/glaucoma, periodontal disease
Vitamin B1 (thiamin)	Sunflower seed, wheat germ, wheat bran, unpolished rice, blackstrap molasses, oats, millet, spinach, cauliflower, Soya bean (dried), avocado	Destroyed by cooking, coffee, black tea and chlorinated water[49]	Detoxifies alcohol	Beriberi (wet): swelling, decreased heart function; beriberi (dry): weight loss, muscle wasting, degeneration of nerves; fatigue, alcoholism, memory loss, diabetic neuropathy, depression, senility, schizophrenia
Vitamin B2 (riboflavin)	Yogurt, broccoli (cooked), almond, Brie cheese, wild rice, nori seaweed, egg, sunflower seed, soya bean, asparagus, collards, spinach, avocado		Helps in detoxification of estrogens via methylation[50]	Cracks or sores at corners of mouth, dry eyes, cataracts, fatigue, acne rosacea

VITAMIN / MINERAL	GOOD FOOD SOURCES	TOXICITY / CONTRAINDICATIONS	DETOXIFICATION PATHWAYS IT SUPPORTS	SYMPTOMS OF DEFICIENCY
Vitamin B3 (niacin)	Chicken, salmon, halibut, cod, dried beans, wheat germ, brown rice, sunflower seed, almond, soya bean, egg	High doses of the supplement can cause a niacin flush with red itchy skin		Pellagra: diarrhea, dementia, dermatitis; high cholesterol, fatigue, hypoglycemia, acne, schizophrenia, anxiety, Raynaud's syndrome
Vitamin B5 (pantothenic acid)	Egg, turkey (dark meat), chicken (dark meat), brown rice, sweet potato, buckwheat flour, soy flour, green peas, cauliflower, avocado		Reduces effects of antibiotics and radiation Helps to make porphyrin, needed for heavy metal detoxification	Fatigue, stress-induced adrenal insufficiency, arthritis, allergies
Vitamin B6 (pyridoxine)	Wheat germ, wheat bran, watermelon, egg yolk, tomato juice, soya bean, halibut, sweet potato, potato, broccoli, brown rice, pineapple juice, walnut	Reacts with L-Dopa for Parkinson's disease Too much in supplement form can cause peripheral neuropathy- numbness and tingling in the extremities Depleted by the birth control pill	Improves functioning of Phase 1 and 2 cytochrome P450 enzymes for detoxification	PMS, nausea of pregnancy, water retention, fatigue, depression, carpal tunnel syndrome
Vitamin B12 (cobalamin)	Clam, salmon, lamb, trout herring, crab, oyster, egg yolk, yogurt, seaweeds: nori, arame, wakame, kombu; marine algae: spirulina, chlorella			Fatigue, MS, pernicious anemia, allergies, acne

VITAMIN / MINERAL	GOOD FOOD SOURCES	TOXICITY / CONTRAINDICATIONS	DETOXIFICATION PATHWAYS IT SUPPORTS	SYMPTOMS OF DEFICIENCY
Folic acid	Orange juice, spinach, kale, romaine lettuce, beet greens, Swiss chard, asparagus, broccoli, egg yolk, beets, wheat bran, Brussel sprouts			Pregnancy to avoid neural tube defects, cervical dysplasia, depression, adrenal insufficiency
Vitamin K	Our own intestinal flora, turnip greens, broccoli, cabbage, green tea, spinach, asparagus, alfalfa, kelp	Warfarin and coumadin may be interfered by vitamin K		Newborns to prevent hemorrhage, nosebleeds, osteoporosis, floaters in the eyes
Bioflavonoids	Lemon, grapefruit, orange, lime, rose hip, apricot, cherry, yam, soya bean, grape, black currant, blueberry, plum, blackberry, papaya, green pepper, broccoli, tomato		Helps in the absorption and protection of vitamin C and stimulates detoxification of toxins in the liver via Phase 1 and 2 enzymes	Low immunity, colds, flus, bleeding gums, nosebleeds, heavy periods
Calcium	Sardine/salmon with bones, collards, spinach (cooked), tofu, broccoli,	Asthma, kidney stones	Removes lead	

VITAMIN / MINERAL	GOOD FOOD SOURCES	TOXICITY / CONTRAINDICATIONS	DETOXIFICATION PATHWAYS IT SUPPORTS	SYMPTOMS OF DEFICIENCY
Calcium cont'd	dandelion greens, blackstrap molasses, almond, dried fig, dried apricot, sesame seed, orange, kale			
Magnesium	Soya bean, black-eyed peas, almond, hazelnut, pecan, brown rice, kidney bean, Swiss chard (cooked), whole grains, chocolate, avocado	Kidney failure Too much magnesium causes diarrhea		
Iron	Tofu, blackstrap molasses, amaranth, beef turkey (dark meat), baked potato, leek, apricot, kale, spinach (raw), pumpkin seed, almond, tuna, pumpkin (canned), prunes, raisins, figs, cocoa powder	Hemochromatosis		
Selenium	Brazil nut, snapper, halibut, salmon, scallops, Swiss chard, oats, orange juice, blackstrap molasses, sunflower seed	Can become toxic with long-term use	Used for detoxification by enzyme glutathione peroxidase Used to detoxify heavy metals: lead, mercury, cadmium and arsenic	Low immunity

VITAMIN / MINERAL	GOOD FOOD SOURCES	TOXICITY / CONTRAINDICATIONS	DETOXIFICATION PATHWAYS IT SUPPORTS	SYMPTOMS OF DEFICIENCY
Zinc	Oysters (eastern), roast beef, turkey (dark meat), cheddar cheese, Swiss chard, rolled oats, pumpkin seed, soya bean, sunflower seed, ginger root	Can cause stomach irritation, if taken on an empty stomach Too much zinc can deplete copper and folic acid	For heavy metal detoxification of cadmium, lead, copper, aluminum Cofactor for antioxidant activity of superoxide dismutase In the prostate, zinc inhibits the function of enzyme 5-alpha-reductase that converts testosterone to dihydrotestosterone that causes prostate hypertrophy	White spots on nails, decreased sense of taste and smell, prostate enlargement, low immunity
Manganese	Whole wheat flour, brown rice, barley, rye, buckwheat, banana, pecan, Brazil nut, spinach (cooked), almond	Too much Mn can deplete iron, copper and zinc	Cofactor for superoxide dismutase synthesis for detoxification in the mitochondria	Arthritis, fractures
Phosphorus	Swiss cheese, sole, tofu, almond, turkey, chicken, egg	Too much phosphorus depletes calcium	Helps in maintenance of the phospholipid membrane of cells to allow nutrients into cells and toxins	Phosphorus deficiency is rare because it is abundant in food
Copper	Rye, Brazil nut, cashew, blackstrap molasses, sunflower seed, mushroom (raw), almond, cocoa powder	See Chapter Five: Heavy Metal Toxicity; Symptoms of Lead Toxicity) Wilson's disease is characterized by inborn errors in copper metabolism	Cofactor for superoxide dismutase in detoxification, helps to detoxify estrogens, removes lead and cadmium	Anemia, low immunity, vitiligo

VITAMIN / MINERAL	GOOD FOOD SOURCES	TOXICITY / CONTRAINDICATIONS	DETOXIFICATION PATHWAYS IT SUPPORTS	SYMPTOMS OF DEFICIENCY
Molybdenum	Oats, buckwheat, wheat germ, lima bean, green beans, lentil, potato, spinach, cantaloupe, corn, apricot, garlic	Competes with copper for absorption	Detoxifies nitrates, a chemical preservative in cold cut meats Detoxifies sulfites, a chemical preservative in shrimp, salad bars, dried fruits such as raisins, apricots, prunes Heavy metal detoxification of mercury and copper	Asthma, dental cavities, cancer, especially esophageal
Iodine	Iodized salt, seaweeds: kombu, arame kelp, haddock, cod, shrimp, halibut, sardine, asparagus, garlic, sesame seed, soya bean	Too much inhibits the thyroid gland	Helps to reduce the conversions of estrogen in the liver to more toxic forms	Fibrocystic breasts, breast cancer, goitre

References

[1] Editors of The American Heritage® Dictionaries. *The American Heritage® Stedman's Medical Dictionary.* Boston: Houghton Mifflin Company, 2002.

[2] Arthur C. Guyton, and John E. Hall. *Textbook of Medical Physiology*, 10th Edition. N.p.: W.B. Saunders Company, 2000.

[3] Weiner, Michael A., and Janet Weiner. *Herbs That Heal.* California: Quantum Books, 1994, 234.

[4] Willard, Terry. *Textbook of Advanced Herbology.* Calgary: Wild Rose College of Natural Healing Ltd., 1992, 135-136.

[5] Morrison, Roger. *Desktop Guide to Keynotes and Confirmatory Symptoms.* California: Hahnemann Clinic Publishing, 1993.

[6] Gibson, Douglas. *Studies of Homeopathic Remedies.* United Kingdom: Beaconsfield Publishers, 1987,158-160.

[7] Worwood, Valerie Ann. *The Fragrant Pharmacy.* Great Britain: Bantam Books, 1990..

[8] Hoffman, David L. *Therapeutic Herbalism.* N.p.: David Hoffman, n.d., 4: 1-78.

[9] Morrison, *Desktop Guide to Keynotes and Confirmatory Symptoms.*

[10] Townsend Letter for Doctors and Patients' Archives. N.p.: ww.tldp.com (accessed September, 2006).

[11] Organic Health and Beauty. N.d.: www.organichealthandbeauty.com/10 commonchemicals.html (accessed October, 2005).

[12] Trenev, Natasha. *Probiotics: Nature's Internal Healers.* New York: Avery, 1998, 32-35.

[13] Marz, Russel B. *Medical Nutrition from Marz*, 2nd Edition. Oregon: Omni Press, 1997, 25-27.

[14] Hoffman, David. *The Complete Illustrated Holistic Herbal: A Safe and Practical Guide to Making and Using Herbal Remedies.* Australia: Element Books Ltd., 1996, 144.

[15] Hoffman, *Therapeutic Herbalism.*

[16] Spiller, Gene A. *Caffeine.* United States of America: CRC-Press LLC, 1998, 148.

[17] Natural Resources Defense Council. N.d.: http://www.nrdc.org/thisgreenlife/0410.asp (accessed March 2005).

[18] Marz, *Medical Nutrition from Marz.*

[19] Hall, Douglas C. *Nutritional Influences on Estrogen Metabolism.* N.p.: Advanced Nutrition Publications, Inc., 2001.

[20] Erasmus, Udo. *Fats and Oils.* British Columbia: Alive Books, 1986, 255-259.

[21] Erasmus. *Fats and Oils*, 246-255.

[22] Gendel, Wayne. "The Power of Water" Forever Healthy lecture presented at The Joy of Health Naturopathic Clinic, Kleinburg, Ontario, 2004.

[23] Gross, Lisa. "The Hidden Life of Bottled Water." *Sierra Magazine*, May/June 1999.

[24] Kaur, Sat Dharam. *A Call to Women*. Ontario: Quarry Press, 2001.
[25] Iyengar, B.K.S. *Yoga, The Path to Holistic Health*. London: Dorling Kindersley Ltd., 2001, 112-115.
[26] Myers, Esther. *Yoga and You*. Random House Canada, 1996.
[27] Brown, Christina. *The Ayurvedic Year*. Massachusetts: Storey Books, 2002, 75, 132, 206.
[28] Thomas Zhang, interview by Dr. Janine Bowring, ND, Toronto, January 2004.
[29] Department of Health, State of Texas. www.1stenvirosafety.com/documents-mosos1/enviro_msos_hazardouschemicals.doc (accessed January, 2008).
[30] Wolverton, Bill. *How to Grow Fresh Air: 50 Houseplants That Purify Your Home or Office*. United Kingdom: Weidenfeld & Nicolson, 2008.
[31] Redwood, Lyn. "Poison in Our Vaccines." *Mothering Magazine*, November/December 2002, 36.
[32] International Academy of Oral Medicine and Toxicology. www.iaomt.org (accessed January, 2005).
[33] Buhler, Donald R, and Cristola, Miranda. "Antioxidant Activities of Flavonoids." http://emt.oregonstate.edu (accessed April, 2007).
[34] Kaur, Sat Dharam, Rose, Robert. *The Complete Natural Medicine Guide to Breast Cancer: A Practical Manual for Understanding, Prevention and Care*. N.p.: Robert Rose, 2004, 92.
[35] Dulloo, et al. "Efficacy of a Green Tea Extract Rich in Catechin Polyphenols and Caffeine in Increasing 24-H Energy Expenditure and Fat Oxidation in Humans." *American Journal of Clinical Nutrition*, volume 70, number 6 (December 1999). http://www.ajcn.org/cgi/content/full/70/6/1040\
[36] Thomas Zhang, interview by Dr. Janine Bowring, ND, Toronto, January 2004.
[37] Bland, Jeffrey S. "Breakthrough Approaches for Improving Adrenal and Thyroid Function" Nutritional Endocrinology lecture presented by Metagenics, Toronto, Ontario, 2002.
[38] Shames, Richard L. *Nutritional Management of Stress-Induced Dysfunction*. N.p.: Advanced Nutrition Publications, Inc., 2002, 2.
[39] Weinstein, Richard. *The Stress Effect*. New York: Avery, 2004, 44.
[40] Hill, Napoleon. *Think and Grow Rich*. New York: Ballantine Books, 1983.
[41] Morrison, *Desktop Guide: To Keynotes and Confirmatory Symptoms*.
[42] Hoffman, *Therapeutic Herbalism*.
[43] Brennan, Barbara Ann. *Hands of Light*. United States of America: Bantam Books, 1987, 49-54.
[44] Walsch, Neale Donald. *A Conversation with God, Book 1*. United States of America: Hampton Roads Publishing Company, 1997.

[45] *New World Dictionary*. New York: Pocket Books, 1995, 312.
[46] Myers, Esther. *Yoga and You*. Canada: Random House, 1996.
[47] Myers, *Yoga and You.*
[48] Padus, Emrika. *The Complete Guide to Your Emotions and Your Health.* Pennsylvania: Rodale Press, 1992, 175-177.
[49] Marz, *Medical Nutrition from Marz*, 192.
[50] Hall, *Nutritional Influences on Estrogen Metabolism.*